HAT

Please renew or return items by the date shown on your receipt

www.hertsdirect.org/libraries

Renewals and enquiries: 0300 123 4049

Textphone for hearing or speech impaired 0300 123 4041

Hertfordshire

D1492711

H46 533 497 X

First published in the UK in 2012 by
Apple Press
7 Greenland Street
London NW1 0ND
United Kingdom
www.apple-press.com

Isbn 978 1 84543 487 8

An Imagine Book
Published by Charlesbridge
85 Main Street, Watertown, MA 02472
617-926-0329
www.charlesbridge.com

Created by Penn Publishing Ltd.
1 Yehuda Halevi Street, Tel Aviv, Israel 65135
www.penn.co.il

Editor-in-Chief: Rachel Penn
Edited by Shoshana Brickman
Design and layout by Michal & Dekel
Photography by Oded Marom
Food styling by Amit Farber

For information about custom editions, special sales, premium and corporate purchases,
please contact Charlesbridge Publishing at specialsales@charlesbridge.com

Mocktails

200 DELICIOUS & ALCOHOL-FREE COCKTAILS

KESTER THOMPSON

APPLE

Content

Introduction

Recipes

Opposite: Pomegranate & Grapefruit (see page 44)

Introduction

What Exactly is a Mocktail?

There are several terms used to refer to a mixed drink with no alcohol. Many use the term non-alcoholic cocktail, although I find this a basic contradiction in terms, as the original meaning of the word cocktail entails alcohol in no uncertain terms (but then again, I still find the term veggie burger something of an oxymoron). Others use the term virgin cocktails, which I personally find quite asinine, and when I really think about it, rather seedy. The exception, of course, is the puritanical offspring of the Bloody Mary – the Virgin Mary (a name that strangely, no one seems to find offensive). I can only assume that the term latched itself onto other cocktails. While I personally favour the term mixed drink with no alcohol, it is unwieldy at best, not to mention dull. And so to the word mocktail, which is self-explanatory, fashionably post-modern and perhaps owes a small debt to Rob Reiner and his filmed mockumentary *This Is Spinal Tap*. There is a problem with the word in that a mocktail seems to suggest that it is a copy of a cocktail. To my mind, this is a very limited concept, and there are really very few (good) mocktails that are just cocktails without the alcohol, or attempts to recreate real cocktails. Indeed, this would be a pretty dull tome if it only led down that path.

So let's say that this book is a collection of recipes for mixed drinks without alcohol. There are obviously an infinite number of these. I mean, anyone can mix a selection of fruit juices together and call it a mocktail–and why not? So what I have tried to do here is provide a selection of recipes and ideas to inspire you to be a bit more creative. Again, you can mix anything together, throw any number of ingredients into a blender and flick the switch, and maybe you'll come up with the best drink ever made. However, I often feel that this mishmash approach is imprecise and leads to a generic taste; once you've mixed orange, pineapple and apple juices with a few berries and a banana, you won't really feel any one ingredient in particular (with the possible exception of the banana). As with cocktails, I prefer to have a definite starting point or a dominant taste to build from. That's not to say the spontaneous blend described above is inferior or not tasty; it's simply a matter of personal taste. I like to build a drink around one ingredient by complementing, moulding and enhancing it as best I can.

It's interesting to note that while the United States and some parts of Europe have a rich cocktail culture, there is some lack of imagination when it comes to mocktails. That's not to say that there are none whatsoever, but sodas and fruit juices tend to be the default options. However, countries such as India, Thailand and Brazil, to name but a few, have been quietly making spectacular mocktails for centuries, using a diverse array of ingredients that make a Shirley Temple seem as interesting as a wet weekend. Perhaps because the United States and Europe have very alcohol-based drinking cultures, non-alcoholic drinks have been rather ignored. But in these days of globalization and other big words, the West has, in the last 20 years or so, discovered the delights and benefits of drinks such as the Lassi.

One non-alcoholic drink we have all come to know is the smoothie, an entity that has spawned an expansive family of drinks. When we think of smoothies, most of us tend to think of blended drinks that contain fruit, yogurt, milk, honey and maybe a cereal supplement. The real definition of a smoothie is actually very loose, and the term can really be used to describe any blended fruit drink.

Acknowledgements

In my years I have gathered, borrowed and lifted recipes from everywhere, and where possible have tried to make them my own. I've made quite a few up myself along the way. It would be impossible to give my thanks and make my apologies to 20 years worth of people who have inspired, taught and helped me, but if you think you may be one of them, then please accept both, and they come with with much gratitude and grovelling.

However, there are some people I would especially like to thank in relation to this tome: Nir Dagan, for his tireless tasting and positive criticisms, Anya and Philippa for their particular brand of encouragement, and special thanks and love to Margaret, who made it possible for me to take the time to put pen to paper, and to whom I owe more than can be spoken. But most of all, I would be a far poorer and emptier man without my family, Yael, Romi, Mia and Alma, who constantly endure my bizarre hours and even stranger concoctions with patience and smiles, and who make coming home at the end of a day a true joy, rather than a thing that should be done.

Ingredients

I genuinely believe that you can't make anything good without good ingredients. This is especially true of mocktails. You can't disguise concentrated juice with alcohol in these drinks, so there is no point in making a drink based on fruit juices if you are not going to use freshly pressed and squeezed juices.

As a general rule, nothing fresh comes out of a can, carton, or bottle. Though there are exceptions to this rule, we'll get to those later.

While the benefits of using fresh produce outnumber the drawbacks, this comes with one or two caveats:

The first is seasonality.
I always try to use local produce when it is in season. It's not because I'm overly patriotic – although there is something to be said for that, especially in these difficult times – but because there's just no better ingredient. Imported ingredients always seem a bit duller, and fruit that magically appear out of season never quite taste right.

If you've ever eaten a strawberry at Christmas, you might know what I'm talking about. It can be annoying to have your ingredients available for short periods of time, but look at it another way – this will keep you on your toes and experimenting, which is a good thing.

thing. Another aspect of fresh local produce is that every piece of fruit has a distinct shade, texture and flavor, as well as its own level of natural sugars and acids. Again, you have to be on your toes and taste everything. For this reason, mocktail recipes are far less exact than cocktail recipes. I suggest you leave it up to your personal taste, and adjust the drinks you're making as you see fit. You can thank your lucky stars that I am not with you in your kitchen, leaning over your shoulder as you make your drink!

Choosing Ingredients

Generally speaking, I think it's fairly obvious that the better your ingredients are, the better your mocktail will be. I have a thing about using fresh, ripe ingredients that are in season. Of course, this is ultimately between you, your integrity, and your taste buds. No one is watching you. But I hope you will learn the difference between what is really fresh and what some stores call fresh. Wherever possible, prepare your ingredients just before you start working. Most ingredients do not like to 'sit around waiting', and oxygen has a detrimental effect on many cut fruits and vegetables and their juices.

Fresh Juices

Freshly squeezed or pressed means freshly squeezed or freshly pressed, not squeezed or pressed, put in a carton with some additives and placed on a shelf for several days. It goes without saying that when juice is called for, it is juice that you have prepared yourself. If not, I don't want to know about it!

Fresh lemon and lime juices are imperative. And by the way, they are not one and the same. Each one has a distinct taste and quality. If you are going to be making a lot of drinks at one time, say for a party, then squeeze a few cups of these juices in advance and strain into a clean bottle or container.

Sugar Syrup

Sugar

There are so many different types of sugar available today – which one you use is really up to you. I generally use natural light brown sugar, but white sugar is fine too. In most cases, the best way of integrating sugar into your drink is to make sugar syrup.

Sugar syrup is a very handy ingredient indeed. I make it with sugar and water in a ratio of 2:1, but the ratio you use may be slightly different. I recommend finding the sugar syrup that suits your taste buds and then writing down the ratio and sticking with it. This will ensure that the flavour of the drinks you make with this sugar syrup is consistent. While plain old white sugar is the norm, you might also want to try making sugar syrup with light brown sugar, as I do. Don't use this type of syrup in every recipe, just where you think a little extra richness might be nice.

Makes about 250 ml

Ingredients
250 ml water
200 g white sugar

Preparation
+ In a small pot, heat the water gently until it is warm enough for dissolving the sugar.
+ Mix in the sugar, stirring well until it is completely dissolved. Do not bring the water to a boil, as this will affect the viscosity of the syrup.
+ Let the syrup cool and then transfer to a bottle. Use immediately or store in the refrigerator for up to 6 weeks.

Ice

Most drinks taste better cold unless,
of course, they're meant to be consumed
warm. Many of the cold drinks in this
book are either blended with ice or served
with ice. I have tried to suggest whether
drinks should be served with ice, but use
your discretion. When adding ice, try
to add it just before serving the drink
so that it has as little time as possible to
melt and consequently dilute the taste.

* I often add ice to the glass after I have
poured in the drink, although this is a
vague rule with many exceptions. Here
are a few tips about all things icy:

* Keep your ice clean, fresh, cold and as
dry (that is, as close to frozen) as possible.

* Use crushed ice for blending, since
this makes things easier for your blender.
Always put the ice into the blender last,
unless otherwise specified, and don't
allow the ice to go above the surface of
the liquid.

* To make crushed ice, you can either
buy an ice crusher or wrap your ice in
a tea towel and smash it with a flat,
wooden kitchen mallet or rolling pin.
(This is a great way to work off anger.)

* Use dense ice cubes for shaking and
serving. Dense ice cubes are preferable to
hollow ice cubes because hollow ice cubes

melt more quickly and can cause your drink to become diluted.

* Consider the mineral content in the water you use to make ice cubes. If a high mineral content gives your ice a particular taste, you may want to use filtered water.

Angostura Bitters

No self-respecting bartender is without a bottle of Angostura Bitters. Originally invented as a medicine for stomach ailments, it has a long, rich and rather interesting history, which is well worth checking out. Angostura Bitters is a key element in several of the great classic cocktails and is actually an **alcoholic ingredient** itself. However, because its flavour is so strong and intense, no recipe ever requires more than a few dashes of the stuff. Angostura Bitters is made up of a secret combination of many herbs and spices, and is regarded by many as Cocktail Seasoning. Just a drop or two from this small distinct bottle can have a dramatic impact on any drink.

Grenadine

This ingredient can be found at every bar worth its salt. Originally made from pomegranate juice, most commercial brands today bear little or no relation to their pomegranate predecessor and are made with high fructose sugars and red food colouring.

Homemade Grenadine

Making grenadine is easy and the flavour is superior to anything you find in the supermarket. If you can use pomegranates that have been pressed by your fair hand, please do!

Makes about 300 ml

Ingredients
250 ml freshly pressed pomegranate juice
400 g sugar

Preparation
+ Combine the ingredients together in a small saucepan. Heat over a low heat, stirring constantly, until all the sugar is dissolved. Do not boil.
+ Set aside to cool, then strain and transfer to an airtight jar with a tight-fitting lid. Store in the refrigerator for up to 1 week.

Equipment

I shall try to be brief. As I said earlier, I'm not going to tell you what to buy. There are blenders, squeezers and juicers for every day of the week! Many of them are described with words such as centrifugal, automatic, hand press, citrus, ejection and power. I will only say these four things to guide you:

*   Start simple and see if this whole mocktail thing is for you. If it is, invest in some decent equipment, as you (and your bank manager) see fit.

*   I've never met a juicer or blender that didn't dribble or wasn't a pain to clean, regardless of what the manufacturer had printed on the box. In fact, the less mess a blender makes, the harder it tends to be to clean. I live in eternal hope of being proved wrong, but so far, I haven't been. You are going to make a mess. So get over it and enjoy!

*   Use what suits your needs – nothing more, nothing less.

*   Keep your equipment in good condition (something that is true of life in general, I would say). 'Dull blades a bad drink maketh', or so the ancient proverb goes. Remember that ice blunts your blender blades quickly, so keep the blades sharp, according to the manufacturer's instructions.

* As a rule, add crushed ice to your blender rather than ice cubes. Also, note that after a few days, fruit and dairy residue start to smell – really smell! So make sure you keep your equipment clean. Equipment that's not clean can quickly turn into a breeding ground for all kinds of stomach-turning gremlins.

Blender

A good blender is not cheap. If you're just getting started with mocktails, something simple will suffice. You'll know when you're ready to upgrade – it will probably be the moment after you throw your old blender against the wall and stamp the life out of it in frustration. Simple or sophisticated, be sure to keep your blender well-serviced and clean. There's nothing worse than a smelly blender. Try to use crushed ice rather than ice cubes, as they will wear down the blades less quickly.

Juicer

There are many types of juice extractors these days, and what you choose to use is up to you. However, remember that a juicer is absolutely essential. Nothing that comes out of a box is freshly squeezed. Freshly squeezed juice is something that comes out of a piece of fruit that has just been squeezed by you, in one way or another, by hand. Personally, I love the old juice extractors that have to be depressed by hand

and can be used for citrus fruits, pomegranates and a few other fruit, but there are also some excellent newer models available.

You will also need a juice extractor for carrots, melons, beetroot, fennel and so on. Cheaper is never better, but at the same time, expensive isn't always better. Ask around and do some research before you buy. Please, please, please – keep your juicer clean!

Fine Strainer

This is one of my essential items. You can find fine mesh, stainless steel strainers almost anywhere. You'll need one with a diameter of about 10 cm (4 inches). A fine tea strainer should do. A Hawthorn Strainer (page 18) is essential if you're using a Boston Shaker (page 18), but it doesn't catch everything and may leave small pips, seeds and ice shards, which can spoil the perfection of a drink served straight up (without ice).

Grater

You'll need a nutmeg grater, at the very least. You'll probably find, however, that a good grater comes in handy for all kinds of things.

Hawthorn Strainer

This is the generic trademark name for the strainer that fits onto the top of a Boston Shaker. It has a spring in the rim that strains for you and allows for a bit of movement should you want to let certain solid ingredients into your drink.

Ice Scoop

You'll waste an awful lot of time scooping ice if you insist on picking up one cube at a time with a pair of ice tongs! Many mocktails include ice – and lots of it – so an ice scoop is rather important. One with a 6-ounce capacity should be fine for home use.

Knife and Cutting Board

You won't get anywhere without a good sharp knife and something to cut on.

Vegetable Peeler

Clearly, you'll need this to peel carrots and similar vegetables before juicing. You'll also want one to make delicately wispy garnishes.

Jiggers (also known as Measures)

I recommend getting a set of jiggers for measuring liquids. Try and get as big a variety as you can, so that you don't have to 'guesstimate' when you prepare your drinks. You'll find that some jiggers have rather strange measurements, 1¼ ounces being a popular one, which are frankly

of little use. I also suggest that you have a measuring jug on hand, as well as tablespoons and teaspoons.

Muddler

Muddling is the technical term for pressing, squashing, squeezing or smashing fruits and other non-liquid ingredients. Every bar stockist sells muddlers. I recommend using a long one if possible, as short ones are sometimes too short to use inside a shaker and you'll end up hurting your fingers. I quite like using an old-fashioned wooden rolling pin (yes, the type normally used by bakers) with no handles. A wooden rolling pin can also be useful for preparing cracked and crushed ice.

Shaker

There are several varieties of cocktail shakers, but I urge you to get yourself a Boston Shaker. Standard shakers have three parts and although they can be nicely designed and pretty, they just don't do the job properly, as far as I'm concerned. A Boston Shaker has two parts: a metal cone and a glass part. Shaken mocktails need to really be shaken, and a Boston Shaker gives you plenty of room for doing this. Three-part shakers are much trickier than they look and once they are full, there's very little room to manoeuvre, especially if you don't know what you're doing. Also, getting the top off a shaker once the metal part is ice cold can be extremely frustrating (not to mention embarrassing!) For more on how to use a Boston Shaker like a pro, see Shaking (page 21).

Serving Accessories

After all the hard work that's gone into making your delicious mocktail, it certainly deserves to be served in style, don't you think?

Attractive glassware

Clearly, the vessel you use to serve your drink in is important. Choose something that works with the flavours of your drink and the occasion.

Napkins and coasters

Cold glasses frost over and drip, so you'll want to serve your drinks with something underneath them.

Cocktail sticks and straws

These add an attractive and practical element to your mocktail.

Paper umbrellas

These aren't necessary but they are fun. Maybe it's time for a comeback?!

Bar cloth

Ordinary kitchen tea towels don't polish glasses well and tend to smear.

Terms
& Techniques

Garnishing

Simply said, garnishing is the decorating of a drink. Always make your drink look as beautiful as possible. It doesn't matter how much effort and love you've put into making a drink; if it looks like a dog's dinner, it's not going to be appreciated as much as it should be.

While many cocktails call for specific garnishes, this is not really so with mocktails. I have given suggestions, but feel free to improvise and be creative.

My main piece of advice is to select garnishes that suit your drink. An olive, for example, would be rather out of place in a sweet and creamy mocktail.

I like to make my garnishes edible when possible, and certainly don't recommend using anything that you wouldn't put in your mouth.

Measuring

I'm a stickler when it comes to measurements of cocktails. However, where mocktails are concerned, you can call me a hippie. Most of these recipes are borne out of trial and error. Change around the measurements of two juices and you have a totally new drink. I like that idea. None of these recipes are set in stone and I urge you to make them your own.

Muddling

It's a weird term, I know, but an important one. Muddling is basically the squashing, pressing and squeezing of fruits, herbs, spices and other solid ingredients, using a muddler (page 18). I urge you to do all your muddling in the metal part of the shaker. You may see bartenders muddling straight in the glass they are going to use; however, I can tell you from personal experience that finding yourself clutching the remnants of what was, just a second ago, an intact glass can be very painful, messy, and more importantly, a waste of good ingredients! Seriously though, breaking a glass you're holding onto tightly is really no fun.

Muddling soft fruits, such as berries, is fairly obvious. Muddling citrus fruit, such as lime or lemon, is normally done with sugar. You're trying to squeeze all the juice out of the fruit while the sugar is working on the skin and extracting all the gorgeous essential oils that are stored inside.

When muddling herbs such as mint or basil, be very, very gentle. Press very lightly and make sure you don't squash the herb. Many herbs release a bitter flavour when squashed and will quickly discolour.

Don't let your face get too close to the shaker when muddling. Getting lime juice, ginger or chilli (especially chilli!) in your eye will make you cry like a very upset baby!

Shaking

As mentioned above, I highly recommend using a Boston Shaker. When doing so, simply follow these guidelines:

* Put all your ingredients in the glass part of the shaker and then fill the shaker with ice.

* Place the metal part on top and tap it down with the heel of your hand so that it is in place and firmly closed. This creates a seal.

* Turn the shaker over so that the glass part is on top. With one hand on top and the other hand on the bottom, shake the shaker while trying to look as cool as possible.

* When you've finished shaking, hold the whole shaker in the middle with one hand, making sure you've got a good hold on both parts of it. Use the other hand to tap the metal part where the glass should sit inside it (this should be about 2.5 cm [1 inch] from the top of the metal part). This breaks the seal and allows you to lift the glass part, leaving everything in the metal part. If the seal doesn't break, turn the shaker in your hand and try again.

* I urge you to practice with an empty shaker as this can be a little tricky to master. But trust me, it's worth the effort.

Straining

To strain a drink after it's been shaken or stirred, place a Hawthorn Strainer over the top of the shaker or mixing glass. Hold the shaker firmly in your hand, with your fore and middle fingers securing the strainer in place. Strain. Again, practice makes perfect.

Double Straining

If you're serving a drink straight up (without ice), you may want to filter out the pips, seeds, small bits of mint leaf and tiny shards of ice that cannot be stopped by a Hawthorn Strainer. When pouring the drink from the shaker through the Hawthorn Strainer, hold a fine mesh strainer with your other hand, between the shaker and the glass, to catch any more bits and pieces. You'll be surprised at what you may find.

You may find that your fine strainer gets clogged. If this happens, simply put the shaker down and stir the contents of the fine strainer with your bar spoon. This is also useful for times when you want to squeeze the very last drops out of some ginger or crushed strawberries.

Preparation

Like a good boy scout, you should always be well prepared before you start making your mocktail. Here's how:

* Have your glass ready.

* Make sure all the necessary equipment is on hand.

* If you need ice, make sure it's ready.

* Have all your ingredients (including the garnish) close at hand. This is less obvious than it sounds!

* When you start mixing, start with the cheapest ingredients first (just in case you make any mistakes).

* Once the ice goes in, know that your time is limited.

* As soon as you've finished shaking or blending, quickly taste the drink by dipping a straw into the contents, covering the top of the straw with your finger, putting the dipped end in your mouth and releasing your finger at the other end. You can adjust your mocktail while it's in the shaker or blender – you can't once it's in the glass!

* **Never stick your hand in a blender while it is attached to the motor. Please! This is the stuff of my nightmares!**

* Pour the drink as quickly as possible. Don't put the shaker down and start wondering, 'Now where did I leave that strainer...?' The drink only gets more diluted the longer it sits in the shaker.

* Don't be upset if the drink doesn't taste quite right, or even if it's horrible. Try to figure out what went wrong and try again.

* The most important thing is to have fun. Seriously, have fun.

Health Benefits

How to Use this Book

There are all kinds of reasons for choosing to drink a mocktail over a cocktail. That said, wherever possible, I will give you a heads up on the benefits or downsides of certain ingredients. Please note, however, that is not a health book. Indeed, some of the recipes are clearly not health orientated! Wheatgrass, for example, is a health supplement, and you won't find any wheatgrass here. I tried it once – never again! Similarly, you won't find any recipes that include vitamin pills.

I am not a doctor. Nor am I a nutritionist or a dietitian. In fact, I am quite the opposite. I am a bartender; someone who has spent his life making people perhaps slightly unhealthier than they were before they met me! Some of the ingredients used in the recipes in this book can have surprising effects on our bodies. If you are in doubt about any of the ingredients, please consult with someone who knows more about these intricacies than I do.

These are your drinks, made by you, for you, your family and your guests. The most important thing is that YOU like them. I would like to think that this book is a touchstone; something for you to dip into for ideas. Try a recipe and then toss the book aside and make it your own. Just remember to write your recipes down. I know from experience that not being able to remember how you made 'the best drink in the history of drink preparation' can be deeply disconcerting.

One more thing – you'll notice that I have rarely specified which glassware to use for which drink. When cocktails are concerned, I am a stickler for serving a drink in its correct glass, but as far as mocktails are concerned, I think it is entirely up to you, the occasion, and what you want your drink to say.

Fruit Mocktails

I sometimes wonder who the first person was who decided to try eating a prickly pear, and why they did it. Picking prickly pears can be agony if you don't do it right, and maddeningly irritating if you do. What possessed someone to think to themselves, "Hey, I bet there's a really tasty treat underneath all those thorns and spines that are clearly telling me to keep away..."?

Spend just five minutes thinking about fruits, in all their weird and diverse shapes and sizes, colors and smells, tastes and textures, and it may just renew your appreciation of the world. It may even make you smile. Huge and tiny things grow all around us, bursting with flavor and nutrition, often full of vitamins, natural sugars, minerals and complicated things like bioflavonoids. I'm most certainly not a biochemist, but the study of bioflavonoids seems to be an ever-expanding one that is full of medicinal potential; the pigments that give fruit their striking color might one day save us from cancer. It is often forgotten, or at least taken for granted, that fruits are also a great source of that most essential natural element — water.

But, as I said, I'm not a scientist. While I'm happy to know that eating and drinking fruits may well be doing good for some reason I am unaware of, I am primarily interested in taste, and there is such an abundance of different tastes in the fruit world that a million recipes would not do them justice. Food and drink companies are eager to tell us that their processed products are full of the natural vitamins and nutrients found in fresh fruit. While this may be so, I remain cynical and suspicious. In my mind, there is simply no substitute for a ripe piece of fresh fruit. I urge you to go to your local market and seek out fresh, seasonal, local produce. Fruit that has ripened at its own natural pace and in its natural climate is the best (and tastiest) fruit. For example, you can probably find strawberries all year round if you are willing to pay for them, but ask yourself whether the strawberries that you eat out of season — the ones that have come from a greenhouse or traveled thousands of miles — are really as tasty as the ones that appear seasonally in the local market. Buy fresh fruit and juice it at the last minute. Relish the flavor, savor the taste and don't hide it behind a million other flavors.

Lemonade

'When Fate hands you a lemon, make lemonade.' Dale Carnegie

Is there any better way to open a book than with a glass of homemade lemonade? I, for one, think not. I just love lemonade. I love its simplicity and how complicated that makes it. In my experience, it is often the most simple recipes that are the most difficult to achieve.

I think this is also true of cooking; what is good Italian cuisine if not the fine art of absolute simplicity? This is often true of life in general; it is easy to hide cracks and flaws with clutter and distraction. If you have fewer ingredients, you actually have a smaller margin for error, and everything is about balance. I've been making lemonade for years, both at home and professionally, for family, friends and customers. And do you know? I still haven't cracked it! There's no definitive recipe that suits everyone.

Ingredients

125–250 ml Sugar Syrup (page 12)
(ml freshly squeezed lemon juice (4–6 lemons 250 ml cold water 1000–750
Ice, for serving
Lemon slices, for garnish

Preparation

+ Mix the sugar syrup, lemon juice and water together in a large jug and transfer to the refrigerator until chilled.
+ Taste the lemonade. If the taste is too strong and tickles the back of your throat, add more water.
+ Serve over ice and with slices of lemon.

Tips

* I like my lemonade tart and use about 100 g sugar for every 250 ml of fresh lemon juice. However, I find about 175 ml sugar syrup is suitable for most people. Try this as you sweeten your lemonade, since you may like it sweeter.
* Always start with less sugar and add more sugar syrup until the lemonade is just right. Remember that it's easier to make something sweeter than less sweet.

Frozen Mint Lemonade

Frozen Mint Lemonade

So, if there were something better than lemonade, then it might just be this. It's very popular throughout the Mediterranean, where mint is used to refresh many a parched mouth. The key to this drink is getting it just slushy enough without adding too much water, which can dilute the taste. If you don't have any sugar syrup, simply dissolve 200 g of white sugar in 125 ml of boiling water and let it cool.

Ingredients

125–250 ml Sugar Syrup (page 12)
250 ml freshly squeezed lemon juice
20 g fresh mint leaves
500–750 ml cold water
400–600 g crushed ice
Lemon wedges, for garnish

Preparation

+ Combine the sugar syrup, lemon juice, mint leaves and 500 ml of cold water in a blender.
+ Add 400 g of crushed ice and blend until the mixture is smooth and slushy. Add more water or ice until the texture is just right.
+ Garnish with lemon wedges and serve.

Tips

* It's easy to kill a drink when blending it with ice, as the ice can end up watering it down too much. So don't add too much water at first, and add more only according to taste.
* Try putting the mint in iced water before using it. This will freshen it up and give it a deeper green colour.

Alternatives

Limes instead of lemons
Both this recipe and the one for Lemonade (page 28) can be made with lime juice instead of lemon juice to make a delicious **Limeade**. If anything, limes are even healthier than lemons and they certainly contain more vitamin C. They were once used by the British navy to ward off scurvy, which is why Americans used to call British sailors 'Limeys'.

Fruits
You can experiment by adding different fruits to this recipe. Be selective though, bearing in mind the mint. Kiwi is a great option.

Shikanjvi

I make Shikanjvi using the traditional recipe and adding a teaspoon of Chaat Masala and a dose of fresh ginger. However, some recipes are as simple as lemonade, with an additional pinch of black salt, rock salt and maybe some black pepper. Other recipes use varying combinations of black salt, roasted black cumin seeds, saffron, black pepper and ginger. I suggest you experiment.

Makes about 1 L

Ingredients
125–250 ml Sugar Syrup (page 12)
250 ml freshly squeezed lemon juice
20 g fresh mint leaves
1 teaspoon chaat masala powder
1–2.5 cm (½–1-inch) piece fresh ginger, peeled and chopped
500–750 ml cold water
400–600 g crushed ice
Lemon wedges, for garnish

Preparation
+   Combine the sugar syrup, lemon juice, mint leaves, chaat masala powder, ginger and 500 ml of cold water in a blender.
+   Add 500 g of ice and blend until the mixture is smooth and slushy. Add more water or ice until the texture is just right.
+   Garnish with lemon wedges and serve.

Pear, Orange & Sweet Potato

Makes 1 drink

Ingredients
90 ml freshly pressed pear juice
60 ml freshly pressed sweet potato juice
30 ml freshly squeezed orange juice
Ice, for shaking and serving
Pear slice, for garnish

Preparation
+   Place the juices in a shaker with lots of ice and shake vigorously.
+   Strain into a glass filled with ice, garnish with a pear slice and serve.

Alternatives
*   If you prefer a slightly thicker drink, don't shake the ingredients in a shaker. Instead, simply pour them into a glass filled with ice, garnish and serve.
*   You can also make a warm version of this drink. In fact, you can even turn it into a soup! Add carrot juice, ginger and nutmeg, and maybe even some crushed roasted hazelnuts or pecans.
*   Fresh ginger only makes this recipe better, particularly in colder weather.
*   If you want to make the taste both sweeter and richer, add a teaspoon of maple syrup.
*   Adding 30 ml or so of carrot juice will lead the drink in an interesting direction.

Berry
& Pomelo

I was playing around with the Mojito (page 36) and ended up with this drink. It bears very little resemblance to the Mockjito, but I started at point A and arrived deliciously at point B after a few detours.

Pomelos, not to be confused with oroblancos (although you can also use them here), are tasty, fantastic and, to be frank, slightly ridiculous. That's why there are a favourite in our house. They are big unwieldy fruits that can weigh up to 2 kg and require a fair bit of skill to peel. However, the flesh is not dissimilar to a non-acidic sweet grapefruit and peeling them is well worth the effort. The red variety of pomelo is even sweeter than the green variety, but juicing them can be even trickier.

Ingredients

Handful raspberries
1–2 teaspoons honey, to taste
90 ml of freshly pressed pomelo juice
30 ml freshly squeezed lime juice, optional
Ice, for serving
Raspberries, for garnish

Preparation

+   Crush or muddle the raspberries, using a mortar and pestle or in the base of a shaker.
+   Transfer the muddled berries into your serving glass and stir in the honey. If the honey isn't liquid enough, add a bit of warm water. Stir in the pomelo and lime juices.
+   Add ice, garnish with raspberries and serve.

Alternatives

*   Lime juice adds a nice tartness that I like, but feel free to omit it if you prefer. You may want to make the drink in a jug and pour it through a fine mesh sieve into the serving glass to get rid of any unwanted raspberry seeds.
*   Alternatively, you may wish to make the drink in a shaker. Simply shake well with lots of ice and then pour through a fine strainer into a glass.
*   There are so many citrus fruits, berries and sweeteners to try – you could be experimenting for months! You could also try experimenting with mint or other herbs.

Lemon Barley Water

Ingredients

125 grams pearl barley

1.5 L water

3–4 lemons

100 g honey or light brown sugar,
    to taste

Ice cubes, for serving

Lemon slices, for serving

Preparation

+   Rinse the barley thoroughly with cold water, until the water runs clear. This step is important, so don't skip it!

+   Put the barley and water in a pan and bring to a boil, then simmer for about 5 minutes, or as instructed, until the barley is cooked.

+   In the meantime, remove the rind from the lemons and reserve for later use. Cut the lemons in half and squeeze out the juice.

+   Place a fine sieve over a large heatproof bowl, and pour in the barley and cooking water. Set aside the barley or discard, and mix the lemon rind, lemon juice, and honey into the cooking water. Cool the liquid to room temperature and then refrigerate until chilled.

+   Pour into a glass with ice, garnish with lemon slices and serve.

Alternatives

Some people say that boiling the lemon rind for a few minutes helps to extract even more of its flavour. If you like, add the lemon rind to the water and barley as they simmer. Of course, this will leave you with some distinctive-tasting barley at the end. This method can be combined with some of the alternative suggestions below.

Other fruits

I'm a big citrus fan. One of my favourite things is the oil that can be extracted from citrus peels; it's amazingly aromatic and packed full of flavour, which is why I like to use it when making lemonade, and is also why lemon barley water is so tasty. So why not try orange barley water, grapefruit barley water, or even mixed citrus barley water? You may need to play with the amount of juice and sweetener, but the essential recipe is the same – simply replace some of the lemons with oranges and grapefruits.

Other flavours

Because this recipe requires simmering in hot water, you can add almost any favourite herb or spice to the drink, especially if you have a malady that needs relieving. Try chamomile, lavender, vanilla or ginger. You will extract more flavour if you infuse the selected flavouring in the water with the barley water as it cooks. But even if you don't, adding the herb or spice to the bowl with the lemon peel will still create a flavourful result.

Cinderella

There are well-known mocktails out there and this is
one of them. It's easy to be dismissive of such drinks,
especially if you're like me – someone who always
like to do things a bit differently. However, it's kind
of hard to go wrong with this drink. It won't offend
anyone (unlike some of the recipes in this book) and
will go down nicely at any occasion. This drink is
great if you are entertaining in numbers. Long, fruity,
sweet, sour and slightly sparkly. I have no idea how
it got its name, but just in case, it might be best not
to drink it after midnight! I generally make this in
a shaker, but you can easily multiply the quantities
to make more than a single drink. If you plan on
doing this, simply combine the first four ingredients in
advance. Only add the ice and soda water or ginger
ale when you serve it.

Some versions of this drink call for soda water, while
others call for ginger ale. The choice is completely up
to you; just remember that ginger ale will make it a
bit sweeter. To make the drink your own, feel free to
replace the juices with grapefruit juice, apple juice,
or another favourite juice.

Ingredients

60 ml freshly squeezed
    orange juice
60 ml freshly pressed
    pineapple juice
30 ml freshly squeezed
    lemon juice
Splash of Homemade
    Grenadine (page 15)
Ice, for shaking and serving
Soda water or ginger ale
Orange slice, for garnish
Pineapple wedge, for garnish

Preparation

+   Combine the juices,
grenadine and ice in a shaker
and shake vigorously.
+   Strain into a glass with
ice. Top up with soda water,
garnish with an orange
slice and pineapple wedge,
and serve.

Alternative

Some recipes call for a few
dashes of Angostura bitters.
This is always a good addition
as far as I'm concerned,
but just bear in mind that
Angostura bitters is an
alcoholic substance.

Mojito

Though I'm not a fan of mocktails that are just 'cocktails without the alcohol',
I do realize that there are exceptions to this rule; more than one, actually!
This drink isn't technically a Mojito because it lacks the rum, and my personal
belief is that cocktails are built around their base spirit and not the added extras.
So let's call it a Mockjito and move on!

Ingredients

1 lime
2 teaspoons light brown sugar, to taste
Handful fresh mint leaves
Ice, for serving
Soda water
Fresh mint, for garnish

Preparation

+   Roll the lime firmly on your chopping board, then cut off both ends and chop it into 8 pieces.
+   Put the lime pieces into the metal part of a shaker or a mortar. Add the sugar, muddle well and then transfer to a tall glass.
+   Clap the mint leaves between your hands to release the aroma and add them to the glass.
+   Add ice and then fill the glass nearly to the top with soda water. Stir and churn well.
+   Top up with ice, garnish with mint and serve.

Alternatives

Sugar

You don't have to use light brown sugar. In fact, when I make a real Mojito, I actually use white sugar in order to maintain the taste of the rum. I prefer brown sugar here, since it adds a real depth of flavour. You can also use sugar syrup if you want, around 30 ml, depending on your taste buds and the lime. Alternatively, you can stir in 2 teaspoons of honey, instead of sugar, with the lime juice.

Lime

I really like to see the lime in this drink, but if you prefer a cleaner, less cluttered drink, you can squeeze the juice from the lime and then discard the shells. You should either stir the sugar into the lime juice and then proceed with the recipe, or use sugar syrup.

Pink Grapefruit & Basil Mojito

Feeling adventurous? Try this: replace the mint with basil and add some muddled pink grapefruit. You can also use try mint and basil together, but I personally prefer to keep my tastes simple.

Pink Grapefruit & Basil Mojito

Red Smash

Makes 1 drink

Ingredients
4 strawberries
8 raspberries
90 ml freshly pressed apple juice
15 ml freshly squeezed lime juice
1 teaspoon honey
Ice, for shaking and serving
Strawberries and raspberries, for garnish

Preparation
+   Muddle the strawberries and raspberries in the base of a shaker.
+   Add the apple juice, lime juice, honey and ice, and shake vigorously.
+   Strain into a glass with ice, garnish with berries and serve.

Tips
*   When straining the mixture into the glass, try to let the flesh of the berries into the drink.
*   This drink can also be made with a blender, but the texture will be thicker. If you're blending the drink, remember to use crushed ice.

Alternative
I recommend experimenting with different types of berries.

Spicy Mandarin

Makes about 1 L

Ingredients
1 L freshly squeezed mandarin juice
½ teaspoon finely chopped chilli pepper, or to taste
Handful fresh coriander
Pinch of salt
Ice, for serving
Coriander leaves, for garnish
Miniature chilli peppers, for garnish

Preparation
+   Combine the juice, pepper, coriander and salt in a jug and refrigerate for at least 1 hour. The longer you wait, the more the flavours will develop.
+   To serve, pour the juice into a glass with ice and coriander leaves.
+   Garnish with miniature chilli peppers.

Spicy Mandarin

Pussyfoot

Pussyfoot

This is another well-known mocktail recipe and one of the better ones. It was named after Prohibition leader William E. Johnson, who garnered the nickname Pussyfoot Johnson because of his agent provocateur tactics for gleaning information about illegal saloons and breweries. He would pose as a keen drinker or anti-Prohibitionist to gain his victim's confidence and later use the information against them.

The Pussyfoot was invented at the Embassy Club in the 1920s and you can find all sorts of recipes bearing the name. Beware: there are many poor imitations, but the drink ain't genuine if it doesn't have an egg yolk. The egg yolk may put some people off, but it changes the drink entirely, giving it a velvety texture and creamy richness that transcends an ordinary glass of juice. It is an excellent pick-me-up.

Ingredients

90 ml freshly squeezed orange juice
15 ml freshly squeezed lemon juice
15 ml freshly squeezed lime juice
15 ml Homemade Grenadine (page 15)
1 raw egg yolk
Ice, for shaking and serving
Lime slices, for garnish

Preparation

+   Combine all the ingredients in a shaker and shake vigorously.
+   Strain into a glass with ice, garnish with lime slices and serve.

Alternatives

*   The big question is whether or not to add soda water to the drink. Some people do and some don't. While adding soda gives the drink a delightful froth and sparkle, I feel that it also compromises the taste and texture that I like so much. I recommend you try with and without soda, and then decide which version you prefer. If you do add soda, use about 60–90 ml of it.
*   Feel free to play around with the quantities of the juices, making it as sour as you see fit. I would warn against using too much grenadine, as this can really kill a drink.
*   Some recipes call for a few mint leaves to be muddled in the base of the shaker before adding the rest of the ingredients. Feel free to try it, but I personally prefer it without. Some people find that the mint gives the drink an interesting tang, but I find it distracting.
*   Replacing the grenadine with honey or agave syrup will give the drink a bit of extra depth.

Big Berry

Makes 1 drink

Ingredients

3–4 strawberries
7–8 raspberries
90 ml freshly pressed cucumber juice
90 ml freshly pressed watermelon
    juice
Ice, for shaking and serving
Cucumber slice, for garnish
Berries, for garnish

Preparation

+ Muddle the berries in the base of
a shaker.
+ Add the cucumber juice, watermelon
juice and ice, and shake vigorously.
+ Strain into a glass filled with ice,
garnish with a cucumber slice and
berries, and serve.

Alternatives

★ This recipe is also lovely with
just one of the two juices, though it
definitely works best when both juices
are combined.
★ Fresh mint leaves are an obvious
extra to this recipe; torn basil leaves
are a less obvious, but equally delicious
addition.

Ginger Ale Bellini

*This is another 'cocktail copy' and an
excellent drink for serving at brunch or
lunch. The original Bellini was invented
in Harry's Bar in Venice in 1945.
I would guess that the first alcohol-free
version was tried pretty soon afterwards.
The original recipe calls for white peach
puree and Prosecco, and many Venetian
bars will only serve Bellinis from May to
October, when white peaches are
in season.*

Makes 1 drink

Ingredients

1 white peach, peeled and chopped
Sugar Syrup (page 12), to taste
Ginger ale
White peach slice, for garnish

Preparation

+ Place the peach in a blender and blend
until smooth. Force the puree through a
fine mesh sieve with the back of a spoon.
Add a little sugar syrup if the peach
puree isn't sweet enough.
+ Fill a champagne glass halfway with
ginger ale. Carefully pour in the peach
nectar, stirring gently and taking care
that the drink doesn't fizz up as you pour.
+ Top up with ginger ale, garnish with a
peach slice and serve.

Ginger Ale Bellini

Pomegranate & Grapefruit

I have prepared this recipe many times and it has always served me well. I'm sure you can tinker with it and make a thousand variations – and so you should! The easiest way to extract pomegranate juice is with a manual juicer or press that has a big handle. It's not easy work, but hey, it's good exercise (see page 5).

Makes 1–2 drinks

Ingredients

120 ml freshly pressed
    pomegranate juice
90 ml freshly squeezed pink
    grapefruit juice
30 ml freshly squeezed lime juice
30 ml Vanilla Syrup (page 154)
½ lemongrass stalk, chopped and
    smashed or juiced
Ice, for shaking and serving
Lemongrass leaves, for garnish

Preparation

+ Combine all the ingredients in a shaker and shake vigorously.
+ Pour into a glass filled with ice, garnish with lemongrass leaves and serve.

Pink Grapefruit & Fennel

Makes 1 drink

Ingredients

5 fresh basil leaves, torn
Ice, for serving
60 ml freshly pressed fennel juice
120 ml freshly squeezed pink
    grapefruit juice
15–30 ml Sugar Syrup (page 12)
Pink grapefruit slice, for garnish
Fennel fronds, for garnish

Preparation

+ Clap the basil leaves between your hands to release the aroma and then put them in a glass. Add ice, fennel juice, grapefruit juice and sugar syrup and churn well.
+ Garnish with a grapefruit slice and fennel fronds, and serve.

Alternatives

* You can shake this drink in a shaker rather than stir it in a glass. However, if you do this, put the basil leaves in the glass before adding the juice, both for flavour and aesthetics.
* As always, fresh ginger could be just the right addition to this drink. If you really want to be daring, a touch of fresh ground chilli adds a distinctive *je ne sais quoi.*

Pink Grapefruit & Fennel

Persimmon & Fennel

Ripe persimmons are deliciously sweet and juicy with high glucose content and a fantastic array of vitamins, fibre and electrolytes. The most widely available species of persimmon are Japanese or Asian persimmons (also known as kaki). The most common cultivars are the Fuyu, which is not astringent when unripe, and the Hachiya, which is astringent.

Makes 1–2 drinks

Ingredients
60 ml freshly pressed fennel juice
120 ml freshly pressed
    persimmon juice
15 ml freshly squeezed lime juice
15 ml Sugar Syrup (page 12)
Ice, for shaking and serving
Persimmon slice, for serving

Preparation
\+   Combine all the ingredients in a shaker and shake vigorously.
\+   Strain into a glass with ice, garnish with persimmon slice and serve.

Tip
You can play with the measurements in this drink, but be careful with the fennel juice as it has a strong taste.

Sangrita

I realize that this may seem a rather odd inclusion, but allow me to explain. Sangrita, which literally means 'little blood', is a Mexican drink that is traditionally accompanied by a shot of tequila. I've been making it that way for some time, but the funny thing is that more and more people are asking for another round of Sangrita.

Makes about 500 ml

Ingredients
1 small Bermuda onion, very
    finely chopped
1 teaspoon very finely chopped chipotle
    pepper, to taste
1 teaspoon very finely chopped Jalapeño
    pepper, very finely chopped, to taste
210 ml freshly squeezed
    pomegranate juice
210 ml freshly squeezed orange juice
    (should be blood orange, but don't
    worry too much if it isn't)
60 ml freshly squeezed lime juice
Pinch of salt

Preparation
\+   Combine everything in a pitcher and refrigerate for about 24 hours.
\+   Serve chilled. If you don't like small pieces of onion or pepper in your drink, blend the mixture before serving.

Sangrita

CocoBana

Makes 1 drink

Ingredients

1 banana, chilled
40 g shredded fresh coconut
(about ½ coconut), chilled
90 ml freshly squeezed orange
juice, chilled
30 ml freshly squeezed lime
juice, chilled
15–30 ml Vanilla Syrup (page 154),
chilled

Preparation

+   Combine all the ingredients in a
blender, blend until smooth and serve.

Alternatives

*   If you can't get hold of fresh coconut,
you could use coconut cream, but it's
really not the same thing. It also doesn't
sit too happily with the orange juice.
*   The blend of coconut and banana
is kind of the epitome of what we call
tropical. You could throw just about any
fruit into the mix and come up with
something interesting. But, again, try to
keep the integrity of your flavours. In the
above recipe, the banana, coconut and
orange are all dominant flavours that
stand up for themselves. If you want
to use other fruits, consider reducing
the flavours.

CocoBana, Apple & Lime

*Bananas are impossible to juice, so
don't even attempt it. This means that
all banana drinks need to be blended
and will have a thicker texture, which
makes them so popular in the world
of smoothies.*

Makes 1 drink

Ingredients

1 banana
40 g shredded fresh coconut (about
½ coconut)
60 ml freshly pressed apple juice
30 ml freshly squeezed lime juice
15–30 ml Vanilla Syrup (page 154)
4–5 strawberries

Preparation

+   Combine all the ingredients in a
blender, blend until smooth and serve.

Alternative

Melon or watermelon would also go
together really nicely, but if you choose
either of these, omit the apple and lime
juices altogether.

Plum Lime Chaat Masala

Indian drink recipes often have taste combinations that may seem alien to Westerners on first sip. While Western drinks tend to focus on sweet and sour flavours, all kinds of flavours are incorporated into Indian drinks to enhance the taste of the fruit and facilitate hydration. Many Indian drinks include chaat masala, a blend of spices that may include garam masala, cumin seed, coriander seed, black salt (Kala Namak), rock salt, black pepper, dried chilli, dried mango powder (amchoor), dried ginger powder, asafoetida and more. Chaat masala can be purchased in spice stores or made at home.

Makes 1 drink

Ingredients

180 ml freshly pressed plum juice
15 ml freshly squeezed lime juice
1 teaspoon honey
1 teaspoon chaat masala powder
Ice, for serving

Preparation

+   Mix together the juices, honey and chaat masala.
+   Chill for 1 hour to increase the impact of the chaat masala on the flavour.
+   Pour into a glass filled with ice and serve.

Aam Panna (Mango)

If you like, replace the mango with banana in this recipe. No need to cook it in advance – just place it in the blender with the rest of the ingredients.

Makes 1 drink

Ingredients

1 medium mango, whole and with peel
2 pinches of roasted cumin seeds
2 pinches of black salt (Kala Namak)
10 mint leaves
Sugar or honey, to taste
2.5-cm (1-inch) piece fresh ginger, peeled and sliced
1 teaspoon chaat masala powder
Water, if necessary
Ice, for serving

Preparation

+   Place the mango in a small pot and fill pot with water to cover the mango. Bring the water to a boil, then reduce heat and simmer until mango is tender.
+   Remove the mango from the water and set aside to cool. Then peel, using a sharp knife.
+   Place the mango flesh, cumin seeds, black salt, mint leaves, sugar, ginger and chaat masala powder into a blender, and blend. If the texture is too thick, add some water.
+   Pour into a glass filled with ice and serve.

Kiwi Ka Panna

Kiwi Ka Panna

Makes 1 drink

Ingredients
2 kiwis
250 ml water
15 ml freshly squeezed lemon juice
2 pinches of roasted cumin seeds
2 pinches of black salt (Kala Namak)
10 mint leaves
Sugar or honey, to taste
2.5-cm (1-inch) piece fresh ginger, peeled
 and sliced, to taste
1 teaspoon chaat masala powder
Ice, for serving
Kiwi slices, for garnish

Preparation
+   Pierce the kiwis with a toothpick and heat in the microwave or oven for a couple of minutes, until tender.
+   When kiwis are cooked through, remove peel and transfer to a blender.
+   Add the water, lemon juice, cumin seeds, black salt, mint leaves, sugar, ginger and chaat masala, and blend until smooth.
+   Pour into a glass filled with ice.
+   Garnish with kiwi slices and serve.

Alternative
If you like, add crushed ice to the blender and serve this as a slushy drink.

Pomegranate & Orange Chaat Masala

Makes 1 drink

Ingredients
120 ml freshly pressed
 pomegranate juice
120 ml freshly squeezed orange juice
1 teaspoon chaat masala powder
Ice, for serving

Preparation
+   Mix together the pomegranate juice, orange juice and chaat masala.
+   Chill for 1 hour to increase the impact of the chaat masala on the flavour.
+   Pour into a glass filled with ice and serve.

Baesook (Baesuk)

Hwachae is a general name for a type of Korean fruit punch. I won't pretend that I am an expert in Korean culture and there is no way that I can do justice to the full tradition of Hwachae, but having tried out several recipes at home, I am prepared to make a fool of myself and guide you in the basic direction of Hwachae preparation. Above all, when made well, certain types of Hwachae are things of beauty, and attention should be paid to how they are served.

Baesook is a popular type of Hwachae that's ideally made with Pyrus pyrifolia fruit, otherwise known as the Asian, Korean or Chinese pear. These fruit can be quite hard to find and their flavour lies somewhere between a pear and an apple. If you can't find any at your local supermarket, you could substitute with two pears, two apples, or one of each. It's common to remove the peel from the fruit, though I prefer to leave it on.

Ingredients

24 black peppercorns
2 Asian pears, cored and quartered
500–750 ml water
2 tablespoons honey
2.5-cm (1-inch) piece fresh ginger, peeled and sliced
Pine nuts, for garnish, optional

Preparation

+   Stick 3 peppercorns into each pear quarter.
+   Place the water, honey and ginger in a small pan and heat gently, while stirring, until the honey dissolves.
+   Add the pears and bring to a boil, then reduce heat to low and simmer gently for about 10 minutes, until the pears are poached.
+   Let the mixture cool to room temperature and then refrigerate until chilled.
+   Transfer the pears and the liquid to a glass bowl.
+   Garnish with pine nuts and serve.

Alternatives

*   This drink can be served hot or cold.
*   Although it's not keeping with tradition, I like to add lemon zest before serving.
*   If the season is right, try substituting the pears with fresh peaches.

Baesook (Baesuk)

Lychee, Vanilla & Rosewater

I have a love-hate relationship with lychee, much as I do with dates (the fruit, not the other type, although having said that...). I always look at them, and think, 'Nah, I just can't be bothered. Too much work and mess for something so small. Rather like eating quail.' But then I have one, and then I need to have as many as I can possibly find! They are so delicious. While the tinned variety can be useful in a bar because of the tasty syrup that comes with the fruit, try to juice fresh lychees if you can. There is a particular perfume to fresh lychees that is like no other. I would also recommend that you avoid blending them, as their strange texture makes for a thick, foamy drink that is not altogether pleasant in the mouth – well, not to me, anyway. In this recipe, lychee is definitely the star. The vanilla, apple and rosewater add aromatic hues, but should not be allowed to compete for the spotlight.

Ingredients

120 ml freshly pressed
    lychee juice
60 ml freshly pressed
    Granny Smith apple juice
15 ml Vanilla Syrup
    (page 154)
Splash of rose water
Ice, for shaking and serving
Fresh lychees, for garnish
Granny Smith apple slices,
    for garnish

Preparation

+   Combine all the ingredients in a shaker and shake vigorously.
+   Strain into a glass filled with ice, garnish with lychees and apple slices, and serve.

Tips

⋆   Rosewater can be very overbearing, depending on the brand and quality. You should be able to find it without much difficulty, particularly in Middle Eastern stores. Use it sparingly.
⋆   You can forgo the apple juice, if you like, which is really here to add a touch of sourness and length.

Lychee, Vanilla & Rosewater

Watermelon & Kiwi Cooler

This recipe is a great example of just how simple and healthy a drink like this can be. Watermelon is an extraordinary source of nutrition. It is high in vitamins A, C, B1 and B6, as well as antioxidants, magnesium and potassium. Watermelon proactively cools you down on a hot day.

Makes 1 drink

Ingredients
1 kiwi, peeled and quartered
50–75 g seedless watermelon cubes
1-cm (½-inch) piece fresh ginger, peeled
    and sliced
30 ml freshly squeezed lime juice
1 teaspoon honey, to taste
Ice, for shaking and serving
Kiwi slice, for garnish
Watermelon slice, for garnish

Preparation
\+ Place the kiwi and watermelon in the blender, and blend until smooth.
\+ Smash the ginger in the base of a shaker. Add the other ingredients (dissolve the honey in a small amount of hot water if necessary) to the shaker and shake vigorously.
\+ Strain into a glass filled with ice, garnish with watermelon and kiwi slices, and serve.

Aromatic Watermelon

This is a simple, perhaps unexpected recipe. It makes a great brunch drink, and I heartily suggest that you try it. In the Mediterranean, watermelon is often eaten with white salty cheese – just an idea for you. I love the combination of watermelon and basil, both in terms of taste and aesthetics. See what you think.

Makes 1 drink

Ingredients
50 g seedless watermelon cubes
5–6 basil leaves, torn
Ice, for shaking and serving
1 teaspoon honey, to serve
Basil leaves, for garnish
Pinch of cracked black pepper,
    for garnish

Preparation
\+ Place the watermelon in a blender, and blend until smooth. Pour it through a strainer to get juice, if you like.
\+ Place the watermelon, basil, honey and ice in a shaker with shake vigorously.
\+ Pour the mixture into a glass filled with ice. Drizzle with honey, garnish with basil and black pepper, and serve.

Aromatic Watermelon

Vegetable,
Herb & Spice
Mocktails

If the world of fruits is weird and wonderful, then the world of vegetables, herbs and spices is downright bizarre! I've lumped them together here for convenience, but what an enormous topic! While fruits tend to be regarded as part of the flowering part of a plant, vegetables may refer to a root, bulb, leaf, stem, beet or fruit. Rhubarb is really a vegetable, although not legally so, and tomatoes are really a fruit, although rarely perceived as such. Sweet peppers are actually fruits too. Be grateful there are no mushrooms in this book, because that would really open things up for debate!

It may seem strange to consume some vegetables raw, while you would never consider cooking others. For example, I doubt many of us would ever sit down to a meal of raw sweet potato and cooked cucumber (which is also a fruit, but never mind). It is simply a fact that the natural goodness inside most vegetables and fruits is highest when it is in its natural, uncooked state. But tell someone you are juicing a sweet potato, and their first reaction will likely be 'What? Raw?' I believe it is simply a matter of habit and perception.

In the West especially, vegetables are often cooked to make them easier to chew, but this reduces their nutritional value, often dramatically. Which raises an interesting question, one which I think many of us would honestly prefer not to consider: Do we eat for the pleasure of taste or for nourishment? Don't get me wrong, I'm all for taste. Unfortunately, sometimes a food tastes better when it is unhealthy! But it is a fact that our bodies need certain things, along with lots of care and attention, and many of the nutrients needed by our bodies can be found in vegetables. There is a misconception that 'healthy = not very tasty' and it is my hope, with this chapter especially, to show that this does not have to be the case. My main concern is taste. Thankfully, the wonderful side effect of most of these recipes is a major dose of 'good stuff' too, which can't be bad.

Beet Mix

I find beetroot to be a great divider. People either like it or they don't, and there is no middle ground. This is even more the case with beetroot juice. Beetroot juice, which is rich in minerals, nitrites and vitamins, has been linked to reducing blood pressure and increasing stamina and is regarded as a great internal cleanser, both of the blood and intestines. However, there a few caveats about beetroot juice. First, you obviously shouldn't wear a white shirt while preparing or drinking it. Secondly, beetroot juice can have the rather peculiar side effect of turning your pee slightly pink – so don't be alarmed! Thirdly and perhaps most importantly, is that it is a really potent ingredient, and not just in terms of flavour. Drinking too much beetroot juice can have some very strange effects on your body. It may cause dizziness, fever, or even an over reduction in blood pressure.

It is often recommended that beetroot juice makes up only one fifth of your drink. This means that if you want the beetroot flavour to shine through, you need to mix it with some fairly gentle companions. However, if you are careful, the benefits far outweigh the drawbacks.

Not only does beetroot juice have a fantastic deep colour, but it also has a delicious sweetness which makes it a suitable companion for both vegetables and fruits. It's a hard vegetable and juices quite easily, giving a good yield. Here are some suggestions.

Beetroot, Apple, Celery & Carrot

For some reason I can't quite explain (maybe it's because of the texture), I like to prepare this drink simply by pouring the ingredients together into a glass. If you like, first combine them with ice in a shaker.

Makes 1–2 drinks

Ingredients
60 ml freshly pressed beetroot juice
60 ml freshly pressed apple juice
60 ml freshly pressed celery juice
60 ml freshly pressed carrot juice
Ice, for serving

Preparation
+   Pour the beetroot, apple, celery and carrot juices into a glass filled with ice, and serve.

Alternative
For a spicy variation, place all the juices in a blender, add some spring onions and small radishes, and blend until smooth.

Beetroot, Pineapple & Cucumber

Makes 1–2 drinks

Ingredients
60 ml freshly pressed beetroot juice
120 ml freshly pressed pineapple juice
120 ml freshly pressed cucumber juice
Ice, for serving

Preparation
+   Pour the beetroot, pineapple and cucumber juices into a glass filled with ice, and serve.

Beetroot, Orange & Carrot

Ingredients
60 ml freshly pressed beetroot juice
120 ml freshly squeezed orange juice
120 ml freshly pressed carrot juice
Ice, for serving

Preparation
+   Shake all the ingredients together with lots of ice. Pour into a glass over ice and serve.

Alternative
Can you hear it? This recipe is begging for some fresh ginger!

Beetroot, Apple Juice, Lychee & Vanilla

Makes 1–2 drinks

Ingredients
60 ml freshly pressed beetroot juice
120 ml freshly pressed apple juice
120 ml freshly pressed lychee juice
30 ml Vanilla Syrup (page 154)
Ice, for serving
Fresh lychees, sliced in half, for garnish

Preparation
+   Place all the ingredients in a cup filled with ice.
+   Garnish with lychees and serve.

Beetroot, Apple Juice, Lychee & Vanilla

Basic Apple Celery

Celery is an extraordinary vegetable. While it is often mistakenly believed that a celery stalk has negative calories (that is, you burn more calories eating a piece of celery than you gain by eating it), it is still ridiculously good for you for many reasons.

Makes 1 drink

Ingredients
120 ml freshly pressed apple juice
90 ml freshly pressed celery juice
Ice, for serving

Preparation
+   Mix the apple and celery juice together and then pour into a glass
+   Filled with ice, and serve.

Alternative
Feel free to substitute the apple juice with pear juice or grape juice. The taste of celery is distinct and is almost always able to climb over other strong flavours, so don't be afraid to experiment.

Apple, Celery & Carrot

Celery has a distinct taste that isn't suitable for everyone. On a more serious note, it can also provoke severe allergic reaction in some people. So if you're planning to serve this drink to guests, don't make the ingredients too much of a surprise.

Makes 1 drink

Ingredients
90 ml freshly pressed apple juice
60 ml freshly pressed celery juice
90 ml freshly pressed carrot juice
Ice, for serving

Preparation
+   Mix the ingredients together, pour over ice and serve.

Alternative
Add the juice of one broccoli stem or a bit of smashed ginger.

Fennel, Lemon & Almond

The unique flavour of fennel makes it a very interesting ingredient to work with. It is rather similar to aniseed, and can be part of some unexpectedly delicious recipes.

Makes 1–2 drinks

Ingredients

1-cm (½-inch) piece fresh ginger, peeled and sliced
Handful mint leaves
120 ml fresh fennel juice
30 ml freshly squeezed lemon juice
30 ml almond syrup
Ice, for shaking and serving
Mint sprigs, for garnish

Preparation

+   Smash the ginger in the base of a shaker.
+   Clap the mint leaves between your hands to release the aroma and add them to the shaker.
+   Add the fennel juice, lemon juice, almond syrup and ice, and shake vigorously.
+   Strain into a glass filled with ice, garnish with mint and serve.

Alternative

For a sweeter version, replace the lemon juice with lemonade.

Fennel, Berries & Lime

I can't resist sharing this recipe with you. It may seem a bit unusual when you read it, but I highly recommend giving it a try.

Makes 1–2 drinks

Ingredients

1-cm (½-inch) piece fresh ginger, peeled and sliced
Handful raspberries, blackberries or strawberries
120 ml freshly pressed fennel juice
30 ml freshly squeezed lime juice
15–30 ml Vanilla Syrup (page 154)
Ice, for shaking and serving
Berries, for garnish
Mint sprigs, for garnish

Preparation

+   Smash the ginger in the base of a shaker. Add the berries and muddle them on top of the ginger.
+   Add the fennel juice, lime juice, vanilla syrup and ice, and shake vigorously.
+   Strain into a glass with ice, garnish with berries and mint, and serve.

King Carrot

Carrot juice seems to have become phenomenally fashionable in the past 10 years or so. There is just a huge chasm between a plateful of chopped, boiled carrots and a glass of fresh, frothy carrot juice. Everyone knows that carrots help you see in the dark (not quite sure how that works, actually), but did you know that they are also full of a form of carotene that the body converts into vitamin A, which makes your liver very happy?

If you eat too many carrots, this same carotene may cause carotenosis, which is harmless enough but may turn your skin orange! Carrots are a good source of fibre and minerals, and have been linked to treatments for cancer and acne, and are used as a supplement for nursing mothers. Most importantly, carotene is good for your hair.

The centre of a carrot can be deliciously sweet, but at certain times of the year, a carrot can have slightly bitter, though not necessarily unpleasant notes, so taste and adjust your recipes accordingly (although you already knew that). The following recipe is now a cliché, but such a good one. After all, it is only repetition that makes a cliché.

Ingredients

120 ml freshly pressed
    carrot juice
120 ml freshly squeezed
    orange juice
1–2.5-cm (½–1-inch) piece
    fresh ginger, peeled
    and sliced
Ice, for serving
Carrot slices, for garnish
Thin ginger strips, for garnish

Preparation

+   Put the carrot juice, orange juice and ginger in a blender, and blend for a few seconds.
+   Pour into a glass over ice, garnish with sliced carrots and ginger, and serve.

Alternatives

*   The juices can be shaken together, if you like, instead of blended, although blending gives the drink a lovely frothy head.
*   You could throw a handful of coriander into the blender as well. Though it may make the colour rather murky, it will also add a very distinct layer to the recipe. Instead of (or as well as) the coriander, try adding ⅓ of a sweet red pepper to the blender.

King Carrot

Parsley & Carrot

Mocktails

Parsley & Carrot

While adding parsley diminishes the vibrant orange colour of your carrot drink, it also adds an entirely new level of flavour.

Makes 1 drink

Ingredients

150 ml freshly pressed carrot juice
60 ml freshly squeezed orange juice
30 ml freshly squeezed lemon juice
15 ml Sugar Syrup (page 12)
Handful fresh flat parsley leaves
2.5-cm (1-inch) piece fresh ginger, peeled and sliced, optional
Fresh parsley, for garnish
Thin carrot strips, for garnish

Preparation

+   Put the ingredients in a blender and blend for a few seconds.
+   Serve in a glass with fresh parsley and carrots strips.

Alternative

I quite like substituting the sugar syrup for vanilla syrup. Give it a try; you might like it too!

Breakfast Carrot

I love this recipe. Simply said, it's a fantastic way to start the day.

Makes 1 drink

Ingredients

2.5-cm (1-inch) piece fresh ginger, peeled and sliced
120 ml freshly pressed carrot juice
60 ml freshly squeezed orange juice
30 ml freshly squeezed lime juice
2 teaspoons quality orange marmalade
Ice, for shaking and serving

Preparation

+   Smash the ginger in the base of a shaker.
+   Add the carrot juice, orange juice, lime juice, marmalade and lots of ice, and shake vigorously.
+   Strain into a glass filled with ice and serve.

Agave & Fruit Margarita

Making a margarita without alcohol can be more challenging than making an ordinary margarita. This version contains lime juice, lemonade and agave syrup. The root bulbs of the prized Webster's Blue Agave, the plant that gives us tequila, are used to make agave syrup. Though agave syrup was thought to be healthier than ordinary sugar for a while, it has since been shown that agave syrup can actually have more fructose than corn syrup. In other words, if you're concerned about your metabolism or your waist line, use agave syrup in moderation.

It's worth adding a note about the salt-rimmed glass here too. When I rim glasses, I prefer to use coarse salts, such as rock and kosher salt, to table salt. Coarse salts have less surface area and a less salty taste, but add a great crunch. However, it is harder to get them to stick to the rim of the glass and they never look quite as aesthetically pleasing as fine salt. The choice is yours.

Ingredients

Salt
1 lemon wedge
1 oz / 3 cl freshly squeezed lime juice
2 oz / 6 cl Lemonade (page 28)
1 oz / 3 cl agave syrup
Ice, for shaking
Peel from 1 orange wedge, for garnish

Preparation

+   Pour the salt into a small plate. Run the lemon wedge around the outside rim of a martini or margarita glass and then dip the rim in the salt, so that the outside edge is coated.
+   Place the lime juice, lemonade, agave syrup and ice in a shaker, and shake vigorously.
+   Strain into the salt-rimmed glass. Hold the peel from the orange wedge over the drink, rind-side down.
+   Twist and bend the peel to release the oils from the rind into the drink, and then serve.

Alternatives

★   This drink can also be served as a long drink in a tall glass, over ice, and lengthened with soda water.
★   Squeeze in the juice from the orange wedge for even more flavor.
★   You can use this recipe to make any type of fruity mocktail, just muddle your favorite fruit and add to the shaker with the lime, lemonade and agave syrup.

Agave & Fruit Margarita

Jamaican Carrot Juice

This drink is simply amazing. You can just use carrot juice if you like, or you can thicken it up by adding some grated carrot for a bit of texture. This is another of those recipes that varies from house to house, so don't be afraid to adapt it to your own taste – that may include adding things!

Makes about 1 L

Ingredients
100 g brown sugar
250–500 ml water, to taste
500 ml freshly pressed carrot juice
2–3 teaspoons nutmeg
2.5-cm (1-inch) piece fresh ginger, peeled
    and sliced, optional
2 teaspoons vanilla extract
125–250 ml condensed milk, to taste
Ice, for serving

Preparation
+   Stir the sugar into the water until it dissolves.
+   Transfer about 250 ml of the sweetened water to a blender or large bowl, and add the carrot juice, nutmeg, ginger, vanilla extract and 125 ml of the condensed milk.
+   Blend or stir until combined, and taste. Add more water and condensed milk, as required. Serve over ice.

Broccoli Cooler

Just the name Broccoli Cooler seems like an oxymoron! Broccoli is a perfect example of something that people would be perfectly happy to eat, yet not prepared to drink, which seems strange to me. I understand that there are different textures and temperatures, but still… Oh well. I hope this drink will convince you otherwise.

Makes 1 drink

Ingredients
90 ml freshly pressed broccoli juice
60 ml freshly pressed cucumber juice
30 ml freshly pressed white grape juice
½–1 kiwi, peeled and cut into chunks
Ice, for serving
Red grapes, cut into chunks, for garnish
Kiwi chunks, for garnish
Cucumber slices, for garnish

Preparation
+   Put the ingredients in a blender and blend until smooth.
+   Pour into a glass filled with ice, garnish with grapes, kiwi and cucumber, and serve.

Broccoli Cooler

Hairy Mary

Pepper & Pineapple

I apologize for the truly horrendous name, but assure you that I didn't invent it. You can add a few dashes of Worcestershire sauce if you like, though I suggest omitting it the first time you try this recipe.

This is one of my favourite taste combinations and I use it in all kinds of recipes. There are all kinds of capsicum peppers, spicy or not, but I think that this recipe is best with good old sweet red bell peppers.

Makes 1 drink

Ingredients
1–2.5-cm (½–1-inch) piece fresh ginger, peeled and sliced, to taste
15 ml freshly squeezed lemon juice
1–2 teaspoons honey, to taste
90 ml freshly pressed tomato juice
90 ml freshly pressed carrot juice
4–6 drops hot sauce
Pinch of celery salt
1–2 pinches of cracked black pepper
Ice, for shaking and serving
Celery stalk, for garnish

Makes 1 drink

Ingredients
150 ml freshly pressed pineapple juice
½ red pepper, seeded and with no pith, freshly pressed
30 ml freshly squeezed lime juice
15–30 ml Sugar Syrup (page 12)
Ice, for serving
Pineapple leaf, for garnish

Preparation
+   Place the ingredients in a blender and blend until smooth.
+   Strain or pour directly into a glass filled with ice, garnish with a pineapple leaf, and serve.

Preparation
+   Smash the fresh ginger in the base of a shaker. Add the lemon juice and then stir in the honey.
+   Add the tomato juice, carrot juice, hot sauce, celery salt and black pepper. Add ice and shake vigorously.
+   Strain into a glass filled with ice, garnish with a celery stalk and serve.

Alternative
To spice things up, add a small amount of spicy fresh chilli pepper.

Pepper & Pineapple

Virgin Mary

Mocktails

Virgin Mary

Makes 1 drink

The Virgin Mary is perhaps the queen of all mocktails and it's as stylish as ever after all these years. The Virgin Mary is, of course, the alcohol-free version of the Bloody Mary, which has at various times gone by the names Bucket of Blood and Red Snapper, and was supposedly invented by Fernand 'Pete' Petiot at the New York Bar, Paris in 1921, or thereabouts.

Ingredients

1–2 pinches of cracked black pepper
1 lemon wedge
180 ml fresh tomato juice
1 dash freshly squeezed lemon juice
4–5 dashes Worcestershire sauce
4–6 drops hot sauce
Ice, for shaking and serving
Celery stalk, for garnish

Preparation

+ Place the ingredients in a shaker, and shake briefly (no more than about 10 times).
+ Strain into a glass with ice, garnish with a celery stalk and serve.

Tips

* Go easy on the spicy condiments. You can always stir in more of your favourites to make it spicier once you've tasted it.
* Celery salt may be hard to find, but it is worth the trouble.

Alternatives

* To make this drink really impressive, pour some salt, black pepper and celery salt into a small plate. Run a slice of lemon around the outside rim of a glass and then dip the rim in the salt mixture, so that the outside edge is coated.

Once you're happy with the basic recipe, give some of these variations a try:
* Add ½ teaspoon freshly grated or creamed horseradish (the latter mixes easier).
* Add some salt or cayenne pepper.
* Add muddled sweet pepper.
* Replace the tomato juice with freshly blended tomatoes.
* Replace the tomato juice with mixed vegetable cocktail.
* Make a **Virgin Caesar** by replacing the tomato juice with clam and tomato juice (often known simply as Clamato® Juice).

Pumpkin Punch

Makes about 1 L

Ingredients

500 ml freshly pressed pumpkin juice
250 ml freshly pressed apple juice
250 ml freshly pressed pineapple juice
1–2 tablespoons honey
2.5 cm (1-inch) piece fresh ginger, peeled
  and sliced, optional
½ teaspoon ground allspice
½ teaspoon ground cinnamon
½ teaspoon ground nutmeg

Preparation

+   Combine all the ingredients in
a blender, and blend until smooth.
Refrigerate and serve chilled.

Alternatives

⋆   If you want even more pumpkin
flavour, add 225 g of steamed pumpkin
chunks to the blender before blending.
This will give the drink more texture and
make it thicker, too.
⋆   Orange juice is another great addition,
but be sure to add it sparingly so that it
doesn't dominate the pumpkin flavour.
⋆   Feel free to replace the apple and
pineapple juices with other juices of
your choice, but remember to keep the
pumpkin front and center stage.

Prairie Oyster

*Here is another renowned hangover cure
and one that should not be taken lightly.
Quaffed by both James Bond and Bertie
Wooster, it looks difficult to swallow
sober (let alone with a hangover), but
is surprisingly tasty and nutritious.
There are several versions, all of them
based on this basic recipe, plus an added
ingredient. Unlike most other drinks, the
manner in which this one is consumed is
very important. Ideally, it should go down
in a single swallow. For the best flavour,
I recommend using Lea & Perrins®
Worcestershire Sauce and Tabasco®
hot sauce.*

Makes 1 drink

Ingredients

1 raw egg
1–2 teaspoons Worcestershire sauce
6–8 drops hot sauce
Salt and black pepper

Preparation

+   Crack the egg into a glass, taking care
not to break the yolk. Add the sauces, salt
and pepper, and serve.

Alternatives

⋆   Add 1–2 teaspoons ketchup.
⋆   Add 1 teaspoon malt vinegar.

Prairie Oyster

Veggie Shake

Makes 1 drink

Someone made this for me once, and I was quite hesitant to try it. But drink it I did, and was pleasantly surprised. Actually, I shouldn't really have been surprised! I'm more than happy to spoon gazpacho into my mouth, so why should it be different to drink it from a glass?

A recipe like this can seem off-putting. Is it too healthy? Is it not sexy enough? I think that if you approach it as a drinkable chilled soup, it may help to change your perspective. We are too sweet-centric in the West, thinking that a straw must be a vessel for sweetness. The other key to this drink is keeping it fairly liquid. Otherwise, it can feel like you're drinking a puree. There are really tasty ingredients here, so there is no reason for it to be dull. I think it needs to be without ice, preventing the flavour from becoming diluted and watery. So make sure the ingredients are nicely chilled before use.

Ingredients

Handful ripe cherry tomatoes
60 ml freshly pressed broccoli juice
90 ml freshly pressed carrot juice
30 ml freshly pressed celery juice
Splash of freshly squeezed lemon juice
½ shallot
Salt and pepper, to taste
1–2 teaspoons honey, optional
Handful green cherry tomatoes

Preparation

+   Combine all the ingredients in a blender, and blend until smooth.
+   Pour through a fine strainer into a glass, using the back of a spoon to help it on its way through the sieve.
+   Garnish with green cherry tomatoes and serve.

Tip

This drink is also lovely when blended. Simply put all the ingredients in a blender and pulse until blended.

Alternatives

If you find that this drink is to your liking, there are all sorts of alternatives that you can play with. Here are some ideas to get you going:
*   Add small piece of fresh chilli pepper, chopped.
*   Add ⅓–½ sweet red pepper, chopped.
*   Add or garnish with 1 tablespoon (maybe more) plain yogurt or crème fraiche.

Veggie Shake

Tropical Watercress

Poor watercress! How many times have you been in a restaurant and been served a dish with a pile of watercress languishing on the side, utterly ignored? This shy little fellow is a ubiquitous plate filler, who is secretly waiting to unleash his full power. Indeed, if you blend him up and stick him in a drink, all his shyness disappears and suddenly his full peppery force is felt! Watercress is bursting with antioxidants and phytochemicals, and therefore gets nutritionists very excited indeed.

The peppery, slightly bitter nature of watercress can put some people off, but again, use it to your advantage.

Makes 1 drink

Ingredients
Handful fresh watercress
120 ml freshly pressed melon juice
120 ml freshly pressed pineapple juice
1 kiwi, peeled and quartered
1–2 teaspoons honey, optional
Ice, for serving

Preparation
+   Combine all the ingredients in a blender, and blend until smooth.
+   Serve in a glass filled with ice.

Sweet Potato Smoothie

It has been claimed that you can live quite healthily on a diet of sweet potatoes. Whether this is true (or even advisable) I wouldn't know, but sweet potato is ranked Number 1 on the list of most nutritious vegetables, published by the Center for Science in the Public Interest. It scored 184 points according to their criteria. The number 2 vegetable scored 100.

Sweet potatoes have it all, including vitamins C, B6 and A (in the form of beta-carotene), complex carbohydrates, proteins, iron, calcium and fibre.

Makes 1 drink

Ingredients
120 ml fresh sweet potato juice, chilled
125 ml plain yogurt, chilled
1 tablespoon peanut butter, chilled
Pinch of salt, optional
Pinch of black pepper, for serving

Preparation
+   Combine all the ingredients in a blender and blend until smooth.
+   Sprinkle with salt and black pepper, and serve.

Sweet Potato Smoothie

Aguas Frescas

Aguas Frescas are found all over Latin America, as well as in parts of the Caribbean and the United States. They are very simple drinks that are made in large quantities and sold in cafés, bars, restaurants and street stands from large vitroleros or glass jars. The basic ingredients are nothing more than water, sugar and a flavour, be it fruit, herb or vegetable. They are tasty, refreshing and uncomplicated. While you can buy readymade mixes from stores, this seems to defy the point to me because they should be as healthy and nourishing as they are refreshing. Let's jump straight in with some examples.

Agua de Jamaica

Dried hibiscus flowers, called Jamaica (pronounced Ha-may-ka) in Spanish, are incorporated in one of the most popular Aguas Frescas, which is my personal favourite. It has a gorgeous deep, vibrant colour and is delightfully tangy. One glass is never enough.

I recently had to make a large quantity of Agua de Jamaica for an event and had the opportunity to ask not one, but two Mexican chefs if they had a recipe. There followed what I shall only describe as a "lengthy discussion", most of which I didn't understood, although I did understand several of the hand gestures. Aside from the passion that the subject invoked, I just love that two people can have such a different way of combining dried flowers with water and sugar. The episode captured rather perfectly what I would say is the mantra of this book: to each their own. I'm sure you could make this better than I do. Just use the written recipe as your base, then close the book and follow your instincts. I don't have to drink it – you do! Below is the recipe I prefer (and the one that I ended up using).

Ingredients

2–2.5 L water
100 g light brown sugar, to taste
50–75 ml freshly squeezed lime juice
100 g dried hibiscus flowers (don't be
    lazy and use tea)
Ice, for serving
Orange slice, for garnish

Preparation

+   Place the water, sugar and lime juice in a pot. Don't use too much lime juice, as the hibiscus is already quite tart. Stir until mixture is clear, and then heat until the water comes to a boil.
+   Remove the pan from the heat and add the hibiscus.
+   Cover and let steep for 20 minutes.
+   Remove the hibiscus flowers and let the mixture cool.
+   Pour into a glass with ice, garnish with an orange slice and serve.

Tips

⋆   Don't be tempted to add too much sugar. This is meant to be a very tangy and slightly tart drink.
⋆   This is another recipe you shouldn't prepare when wearing a white shirt or fancy clothes!

Agua de Pepino

Agua de Pepino

Not all cucumbers are created equal. Some cucumbers are tastier than others, and some people like "bigger tastes" than others. It may seem that you need a lot of cucumber, but I find that you need at least equal parts cucumber to water to get a really flavoursome drink.

Makes about 1 L

Ingredients
1 L water
460 g chopped cucumbers
100 g sugar
20 g fresh mint leaves, optional
125 ml freshly squeezed lime juice
Ice, for serving
Mint sprigs, for garnish
Cucumber slice, for garnish

Preparation
+   Place 125 ml of the water and 115 g of the chopped cucumber in a blender, and blend until combined. Add the rest of the chopped cucumber, 115 g at a time, blending between each addition until the mixture is pureed.
+   Add more water if necessary.
+   Add the sugar and mint, and blend to combine. Strain into a pitcher and add the rest of the water and the lime juice.
+   To serve, pour into a glass filled with ice and garnish with mint and a cucumber slice.

Agua de Sandia

Here's a delicious summery drink. For just the right flavour, make sure you use a ripe juicy watermelon.

Makes 2 L

Ingredients
1.5–2 L water
150 g chopped watermelon
100 g sugar, to taste

Preparation
+   Place 250 ml of the water and 75 g of the watermelon in a blender.
+   Blend until smooth and then transfer to a pitcher.
+   Place another 250 ml water and the remaining 75 g of watermelon in the blender.
+   Blend until smooth and then transfer to a pitcher.
+   Mix the rest of the water into the pitcher and stir in sugar to taste.
+   Chill before serving.

Dairy
Mocktails

Human beings have been consuming dairy products for about ten thousand years, give or take a few. Dairy products are used as a dietary supplement and are a fundamental part of many cuisines in cultures the world over. Today, debate rages about the health benefits and dangers of consuming dairy products. Many people have lactose intolerance, which is either an infirmity or the way that the human body is supposed to respond to dairy products, depending on how you look at it. I have no intention of getting into this debate. I love dairy products. There, I've said it. I'm aware of the benefits as well as the risks, and believe I'm mature enough to consume a reasonable and safe amount, as and when I choose.

I believe that if you are capable of reading this book without assistance, then you are wise enough to know that some of these recipes are not going to help you lose weight, while others may. Some drinks should be consumed once in a while, as a treat or when you just feel like being naughty. There are others recipes that you may decide to make a part of your regular diet.

I hope you will enjoy discovering recipes from far away as much as I have, and still do. I also hope you will get to like some recipes that may surprise you, and may even look weird on paper. I urge you to try everything once. Indian tastes may be totally new to your taste buds, but you'll never know if you like them until you try them. If you find you do like them, great! If you don't, don't dismiss the drink and forget about it. Indeed, this is true of all the recipes in this book – and with every recipe you ever read. Years of making drinks has taught me that a drink I don't like is just as important as one I do like, if not more so.

If I like a drink, then I know it's there, and I can always come back to it. A drink I don't like is a type of challenge; something to be understood. Why don't I like it? Did I do something wrong? Did I misread the recipe? Is there an ingredient I don't like? Is it a new ingredient? Can I make the recipe without that ingredient, and will it be better? What was it that caused such a bad taste, and how can I avoid doing it again? Or, of course, you can also just toss the drink down the drain, and turn the page, if you like! It's totally up to you.

Batida

I know I ranted and raved about mocktails that are cocktails without the alcohol, and here I am writing about it. Well, try one of these and you'll see why. I'm not going to pretend that these recipes are especially healthy. Condensed milk has a fair bit of sugar and fat, although I like to kid myself that I'm balancing this out by consuming fresh fruit at the same time. I'll leave that dilemma up to you.

Batidas are a Brazilian family of cocktails, usually made with a local rum called Cachaca, fresh fruit, condensed milk and ice. Obviously, we're forgoing the rum in these recipes, which means you can drink them first thing in the morning! Just remember that if you do order one in a bar, it will come with alcohol! They're very simple and devilishly delicious. You can make a Batida from almost any fruit – believe me, I've tried. If you're going to experiment, be aware that some fruits need additional liquid; otherwise your drink will turn out sludgy and thick. Try mixing fruits with some of their extracted juice, or use a neutral juice, like apple. Alternately, a splash of regular milk will suffice in some cases. Be careful not to use too much ice – add just enough to reach the surface of the liquid you're blending, but no more. Too much ice will make the drink too thick and detract from the taste. Despite the sweetness of condensed milk, you may find that you need to add more sugar to help bring out the flavour of a shy fruit. Make your drink, taste it, and then add a dash of sugar syrup if you feel it is necessary.

I hope no one minds my calling these drinks Batidas, even though strictly speaking, they are not, and should not be confused with their alcoholic parents. Below are some recipe suggestions, but go crazy. Again, there are very few fruits that wouldn't work for this recipe, although you might find that fruits of a more delicate nature, such as figs, will struggle to find their place with condensed milk. If you refer to the recipe for Café Bon Bon Style (page 135), you will notice that it is essentially a Coffee Batida. All of the following recipes are for one drink. You can double the amounts to make two drinks at a time, but don't try to make more than that.

Batida Maracuja (Passion Fruit)

This is one of the most popular and well-known Batidas.

Makes 1 drink

Ingredients
2 passion fruit, cut in half
60 ml condensed milk
Splash of freshly pressed apple
    juice, optional
Crushed ice, for blending

Preparation
+   Scoop the flesh of the passion fruit and place it in a blender. Set aside a bit of the fruit for garnish.
+   Add the condensed milk, apple juice and crushed ice, and then blend until smooth.
+   Garnish with pieces of passion fruit and serve.

Batida de Coco (Coconut)

To give this drink a nutty texture and taste, throw in a small handful of unsalted peanuts.

Makes 1 drink

Ingredients
60 ml coconut milk
2 tablespoons shredded fresh coconut
60 ml condensed milk
Pinch of salt
Crushed ice, for blending

Preparation
+   Place all the ingredients in a blender, blend until smooth and serve.

Apple & Hazelnut Batida

If you like, replace the hazelnut syrup with a handful of hazelnuts and a pinch of salt. You may want to add a touch of sugar, too.

Makes 1 drink

Ingredients
½ Granny Smith apple, cored
   and chopped
60 ml freshly pressed apple juice
60 ml condensed milk
15 ml hazelnut syrup
Crushed ice, for blending

Preparation
+   Place all the ingredients in a blender, blend until smooth and serve.

Batida de Milho Verde (Sweet Corn)

*Try this – at least once!
The amount of sugar you'll add, if any, depends entirely on the sweetness of the corn.*

Makes 1 drink

Ingredients
40 g sweet corn
60 ml condensed milk
Splash of milk
Pinch of salt
Sugar, to taste
Crushed ice, for blending

Preparation
+   Place all the ingredients in a blender, blend until smooth and serve.

Batida de Milho Verde (Sweet Corn)

Piña Colada #1

Makes 1 drink

Ingredients
Toasted coconut
Slice of pineapple
120 ml freshly pressed
    pineapple juice
60 ml cream of coconut
Crushed ice, for blending
Toasted coconut slice, for garnish
Pineapple leaf, for garnish

Preparation
+ Pour the toasted coconut in a small plate. Run a slice of pineapple around the outside rim of a glass and then dip the rim in the toasted coconut, so that the outside edge is coated.
+ Place the pineapple juice, cream of coconut and ice in a blender, and blend until smooth.
+ Pour into the prepared glass, garnish with a toasted coconut slice and a pineapple leaf, and serve.

Alternatives
* If you can't find cream of coconut, use 60 ml of condensed milk and 60 ml coconut milk instead. Obviously, the drink it produces will be slightly larger.
* Although it wouldn't be a true Piña Colada, I heartily recommend throwing in some fresh pineapple chunks.

Piña Colada #2

Makes 1 drink

Ingredients
120 ml freshly pressed pineapple juice
60 ml cream of coconut
25 g fresh pineapple chunks
Small handful unsalted, shelled peanuts
Pinch of salt
1-cm (½-inch) piece fresh ginger, peeled
    and sliced, optional
Crushed ice, for blending
Pineapple slice, for garnish

Preparation
+ Place all the ingredients in a blender, blend until smooth and serve.
+ Garnish with a pineapple slice (and a paper umbrella – go on!) and serve.

Alternatives
* Some people find that adding a banana to either recipe is a great idea. In fact, if you like, you can omit the pineapple altogether and just use banana. In that case, I recommend using condensed milk and coconut milk rather than cream of coconut, since cream of coconut is rather thick and doesn't go well with bananas.
* If the mixture is still too thick, try adding a dash of pineapple juice to loosen it up a bit.

Piña Colada

Lassis

The Lassi has been consumed in India for generations and there are countless delicious recipes for it. Traditional Indian recipes, specifically Punjabi ones, tend to be savoury, combining yogurt with salt, spice and water. They are often served as part of religious rituals or for medicinal purposes. Similar drinks can be found all over the Middle East. The savoury Lassi is a great way to hydrate and an excellent cooling accompaniment to spicy food. It is also a great aid in digestion.

The sweeter kind of Lassi, also available across India, has been more readily embraced in the West than its savoury counterpart, and has become quite stylish. A fashion that consists of yogurt and fresh fruit is not a bad one – and it's rather inexpensive to boot.

Yogurt comes with varying levels of fat content and has many benefits. It has high levels of protein and calcium, as well as vitamins B6 and B12. Often people who are lactose intolerant find they can tolerate yogurt because of its reduced lactose content. Yogurt is also considered to be a cooling substance, a trait that is of paramount importance for those living in hot climates. Furthermore, although people commonly (and mistakenly) believe that water is the perfect antidote to spicy food, yogurt is actually much better at this task.

The Lassi has a rich history and significance, something of a mini culture (pun intended) all of its own. If you're interested, go ahead and do some research. In many parts of India, the Lassi is made with water and buffalo milk. Below, you'll find both traditional savoury recipes and newer, sweeter styles. There are all kinds of recipes, so I've given the simplest form of the recipe first, and then added ideas for optional extras from which you can pick and choose. While savoury Lassis may seem a bit odd at first glance, approach them with an open mind. You might just discover an entirely new taste experience!

Lassi is often made with buttermilk rather than yogurt. It is probably healthier to use low-fat yogurt, although I always find that version less tasty. I'll leave that dilemma for you.

Namkeen

Meethi (Sweet)

This is one of the most traditional types of Lassi. There are various versions of it, but the basic premise is the same. Take note – not a grain of sugar in sight. This drink is commonly made with water, though you can use milk if you like. Note that the cumin is critical to this drink. For best flavour, roast whole cumin seeds in a pan (add a bit of oil or ghee if you like) and grind before adding it to the recipe.

Here's a basic sweet Lassi recipe that's really easy to vary. Try some of the options suggested below or use your imagination.

Makes 1 drink

Ingredients
250 ml plain yogurt
125 ml water or milk
50 g sugar or honey, or to taste
Ice, for serving

Preparation
+   Place the yogurt, water, and sugar in a blender, and blend until smooth.
+   Serve in a glass over ice.

Makes 1 drink

Ingredients
250 ml plain yogurt
125–250 ml water or milk
¼–½ teaspoon roasted ground cumin
¼ teaspoon cracked black pepper
Salt, to taste
Ice, for serving

Preparation
+   Place the yogurt, water, cumin, pepper and salt in a blender and blend until smooth.
+   Serve in a glass over ice.

Alternative
If you're a fan of mint, tear up some mint leaves and add them as well. If you do this, make sure you add the leaves after the other ingredients have been blended.

Alternatives
Love the basic version? Then try it again, with any of these additions:
*   Rose water
*   A pinch of saffron, soaked in the water or milk for 10 minutes before you prepare the drink
*   Cardamom powder
*   Vanilla extract
*   Crushed almonds
*   Malai (clotted cream)

Adrak Ki (Ginger)

This drink can be made either sweet or savoury. While the savoury version may be more traditional, I prefer it a bit sweet, as it really brings out the ginger.

Savoury

Makes 1 drink

Ingredients

250 ml plain yogurt
125–250 ml water or milk
2.5 cm (1-inch) piece fresh ginger, peeled
  and sliced
¼–½ teaspoon roasted ground cumin
¼ teaspoon cracked black pepper
Pinch of salt
Ice, for serving

Preparation

+   Place all the ingredients in a blender, and blend until smooth.
+   Serve in a glass over ice.

Sweet

Makes 1 drink

Ingredients

250 ml plain yogurt
125–250 ml water or milk
1-cm (½-inch) piece fresh ginger, peeled
  and sliced
¼–½ teaspoon roasted ground
  cumin, optional
¼ teaspoon cracked black pepper
2 teaspoons sugar, or to taste
¼ teaspoon ground cardamom, optional
Ice, for serving

Preparation

+   Place all the ingredients in a blender, and blend until smooth.
+   Serve in a glass over ice.

Alternative

Like your drinks spicy? Try adding a bit of fresh chilli before blending.

Ayran

Ayran is a very simple drink, which is so popular in Turkey that it's even served at McDonald's! Still, even with simple recipes there is lots of room for experimenting by using different types of yogurt, such as goat or ewe yogurt. As with the Lassi, the ratio of water to yogurt is ultimately in the hands of the maker. Make sure that you blend the drink for a full minute, since the foam produced by blending is one of the drink's distinctive features. Also, notice that unlike the Lassi, this drink doesn't contain any ice.

Makes 1 drink

Ingredients
250 ml plain yogurt
75 ml chilled water
Salt, to taste

Preparation
+ Place all the ingredients in a blender, blend for 1 minute and serve.

Alternative
Add some mint leaves to the blender.

Doogh

Doogh is a Persian beverage that's popular in Iran and Afghanistan. There are a few different versions, but the key difference is whether or not you make it with sparkling water. Some recipes call for the use of pennyroyal, a minty plant whose leaves are used fresh or dried in cooking. Pennyroyal essential oil can be highly toxic if ingested.

Makes 1 drink

Ingredients
250 ml plain yogurt
1 teaspoon fresh or dried mint
1 teaspoon fresh or dried pennyroyal
250 ml water, sparkling or still
Salt, to taste
Ice for serving, optional
Mint sprigs, for garnish

Preparation
+ Pour the yogurt into your glass or pitcher, and mix in the herbs.
+ Slowly add the water, stirring all the time.
+ Add salt and ice, garnish with mint and serve.

Alternative
Add 60 g chopped cucumber or a bit of cracked black pepper, to taste.

Fruit Lassis

It's easy to understand the growing popularity of fruit Lassis. They're relatively easy to make, tasty and filling. If you minimize the sugar content, they're healthy too. Personally, I would take a Lassi over a commercially made fruit yogurt any day. I'm not going to recommend any particular yogurt – you know what you like – so choose your favourite, whether it's fat-free, Greek or Balkan style. There are no rules when it comes to making Lassis, but there are a few things you should consider:

*   Use seasonal fruit if you can. If it's at its optimum natural sweetness, you won't have to add extra sugar or sweeteners.

*   Lassis are best when consumed immediately after they are made. Don't let a Lassi sit around.

*   Think about whether you want to blend your fruit or muddle it. Fruits like apples and lychees have a strange texture when blended. Personally, I prefer chunky Lassis that contain bite-size lumps of fruit to nibble – but that's me. Fruits like mango and banana are probably better blended, so that their flavour is imparted into the yogurt. Experiment with different methods for various fruits until you find the method you like best.

*   I prefer to make Lassis without ice. This means all the ingredients should be chilled in advance. Generally speaking, this isn't difficult. Obviously, if you prefer ice, then add it! If you don't add ice, you may want to add a little water or fruit juice, especially if you're using thick yogurt, so that you get a drink and not a dip.

*   Try different sweeteners, not just sugar. For example, you can use fruit syrups, honey or maple syrup. Sometimes I like to make Lassis less sweet and then drizzle honey into the finished drink. It looks great (in a messy kind of a way) and I like the surprise of suddenly getting an extra dose of honey.

You'll find some suggested recipes in the coming pages, but as I said, there aren't any rules, so just have fun.

Apple & Hazelnut Lassi

As you may have noticed, I love this combination of flavours! If you don't want to use real hazelnuts, you can use hazelnut syrup instead of sugar. You need to get the timing right here – either smash everything by hand or use a blender. If you use a blender, use the pulse setting and pulse the mixture in short bursts.

Makes 1 drink

Ingredients
150 ml plain yogurt
30–60 ml freshly pressed apple juice
Small handful shelled, unsalted, roasted hazelnuts
15–30 ml Sugar Syrup (page 12), honey or hazelnut syrup
½–1 Granny Smith apple, cored and cut into chunks
Granny Smith apple slice, for garnish

Preparation
+   Put the yogurt, apple juice, hazelnuts and sugar syrup into a blender. Blend the ingredients together in pulses, until combined. Make sure you don't overblend, as this drink shouldn't be smooth.
+   Place the apple in a shaker and smash. Mix the smashed apple into the blended drink and then pour into a glass. Garnish with an apple slice and serve.

Strawberry & Vanilla Lassi

I don't think I need to say much about this glorious combination. Add even more strawberries, if you like. If you're not using vanilla syrup, then add a few drops of vanilla extract to add a vanilla flavour.

Makes 1 drink

Ingredients
150 ml plain yogurt
30–60 ml water, optional
200 g hulled strawberries
15–30 ml Sugar Syrup (page 12), Vanilla Syrup (page 154), or honey
A few drops vanilla extract, optional
Strawberry slices, for garnish
Mint sprigs, for garnish

Preparation
+   Place all the ingredients in a blender, and blend until smooth.
+   Transfer to a serving glass, garnish with strawberry slices and mint, and serve.

Alternative
If you want to be wonderfully decadent, replace the water with double cream.

Cherry Lassi

Your cherries will have to be perfectly ripe for this recipe to work. I am generally not crazy about maraschino cherries, although there are some sublime (and outrageously expensive) Italian brands on the market. But you might consider using maraschino cherry syrup as an optional ingredient. It has a kind of marzipan taste that can add an interesting note to your drink.

Makes 1 drink

Ingredients
150 ml plain yogurt
30–60 ml water, optional
200 g pitted cherries, or more to taste
15–30 ml Sugar Syrup (page 12),
    Vanilla Syrup (page 154) or honey
A few drops maraschino cherry syrup
Cherries, for garnish

Preparation
+   Place the ingredients in a blender, and blend until smooth.
+   Garnish with cherries and serve.

Cucumber & Mango Lassi

Makes 1 drink

Ingredients
150 ml plain yogurt
30–60 ml water
200 g fresh mango chunks
Handful fresh mint leaves, optional
15–30 ml Sugar Syrup (page 12)
    or honey
13-cm (5-inch) piece cucumber, roughly
    chopped
Long cucumber strips, for garnish

Preparation
+   Put the yogurt, water, mango, mint and sugar syrup in a blender, and blend until smooth.
+   In the meantime, smash the cucumber in the base of a shaker. Make sure it's really broken up.
+   Add the cucumber to the blender and blend for about 1 second. You want to mix in the cucumber without pureeing it. Alternately, add the contents of the blender to the shaker, and stir well.
+   Pour the mixture into a glass, garnish with cucumber strips and serve.

Alternative
You can blend the whole recipe if you like, but I prefer it a bit chunky. If you add the mint, make sure you don't add too much, as it could overpower the mango.

Cucumber & Mango Lassi

Rhubarb Fool Lassi

Rhubarb Fool Lassi

Makes 1 drink

This is an adaptation of a classic English dessert. The rhubarb must be cooked before using it. While roasting it is one option, I prefer stewing it with some sugar and orange zest. The liqueur that remains after cooking can also be added to the recipe.

Ingredients

90 ml plain yogurt
60 ml double cream
250 ml stewed rhubarb, or more to taste
30 ml honey or rhubarb liqueur
    (from stewing)
Rhubarb stalks, for garnish

Preparation

+   Place all the ingredients in a blender, and blend until smooth.
+   Garnish with rhubarb stalks and serve.

Alternatives

As you see, you can make a Lassi with almost anything. While there's absolutely nothing wrong with a straightforward fruit Lassi, it's sometimes nice to experiment. Here are a few ideas to get you going, but they're just ideas. Experiment!

*   Passion fruit and kiwi
*   Roasted pineapple with brown sugar and sesame
*   Pineapple and sweet pepper
*   Banana, milk, and spices (cinnamon, nutmeg, ginger, etc.)
*   Lychee and vanilla
*   Chocolate and chilli (Weird? Yes, but tasty too!)
*   Watermelon, mint and basil
*   Carrot and ginger (just use carrot juice, or it will really be too thick)
*   A real Fool includes whipped egg whites, which makes for a wonderful fluffy texture. It's not necessary here, but is definitely worth giving a try. Whip the egg white separately, and then fold it into the drink just before serving.
*   We haven't mentioned ginger for while... How about spicy rhubarb? Mmmmmm, yummy!

Sahlab with Corn Starch

Traditional sahlab is made with flour made from the dried tubers of the Orchis genus of orchids. This type of flour can be rather hard to find, and corn flour makes a fair alternative. I use coconut in my recipe, although you can leave it out if you want.

Ingredients
150 g corn flour
250 ml water
1 L milk
One 250 ml can coconut milk
20 g desiccated coconut
65–100 g sugar
2 teaspoons vanilla extract
3 teaspoons rosewater
Cinnamon or nutmeg, for garnish
Chopped pistachio nuts or almonds,
    for garnish

Preparation
+   Put the corn flour in a medium bowl and gradually add 250 ml of water, stirring until smooth.
+   Transfer the corn starch mixture to a small saucepan and add the milk, coconut milk, coconut, sugar, vanilla and rosewater.
+   Heat over low heat, stirring constantly, until mixture thickens and steam starts to rise. Do not let the mixture boil. This can take up to 1 minute, so don't rush things, and keep stirring.
+   When mixture is thick and warm enough, remove from the heat and pour into heatproof glasses.
+   Garnish with cinnamon and chopped pistachios or almonds.

Alternatives
*   In Egypt, chocolate syrup or honey is often dribbled around the insides of the glass before the warm sahlab is added. This makes the drink even more decadent.
*   If you reduce the amount of sugar in the recipe as you cook the sahlab, you could drizzle maple syrup around the inside of the glass.
*   If you have time, roast some almonds and sugar together in a pan to make a simple almond brickle. Smash the brickle when it cools, and sprinkle it on top of the sahlab as a garnish.
*   Banana lovers might find this a great opportunity to add a banana. You could chop up a banana and add it to the sahlab while it cooks.

Sahlab with Corn Starch

Milkshakes

Milkshakes are surprisingly complicated things. Indeed, the very term milkshake is far too narrow to encompass the huge array of beverages that call themselves milkshakes! There is more than enough material to write a separate and lengthy book only on this subject, however, I've made a tough executive decision on the matter. This book is for home use and one of my hopes is that, more than anything, it will serve as inspiration for you to go and find or invent bigger and better recipes. Most of us don't have the necessary equipment to make diner-style milkshakes, although it's possible to come pretty close. Furthermore, milkshakes are another one of those drinks that can be made with an endless variety of ingredients. So I will try and keep this simple and give you some basic recipes, as well as a few more interesting ones, in the hope that it will provide you with a few ideas for getting started

As I see it, there are three categories of mainstream milkshake recipes. The first category includes recipes containing milk and something to flavor it (in my mind, just milk and flavored syrup is not really a milkshake, but maybe I'm just being a snob). The second category of recipes includes ice cream. The third includes everything that differs from the previous two! An example of this could actually be the Batidas that appear earlier in this book. But I digress. Let's jump straight in!

Tips

These recipes are all for one drink.

I don't think that milkshakes should be served on ice, so make sure your ingredients are pre-chilled. Since we're talking about ice cream and milk, I hope this is quite obvious!

Some people add ice to the blender to make their milkshake thicker. Although there are several exceptions, I'm not a big fan of this. As always, I'll leave the choice up to you.

If you are going to use ice cream, the truth is that full-fat versions make better milkshakes than low-fat versions. The same goes for milk. Some people add corn oil or other forms of fat to their milkshakes, since fat works as an emulsifier which makes the drink creamier. Again, I'll leave this for you to figure out!

Some people swear by malted milk and there is definitely something to be said for the extra richness that 1 teaspoon of malt provides in a single milkshake. Malt extract is sold at many grocery stores. If it's good enough for Tigger and Roo, it's good enough for me!

Take some time to figure out just how big your glass is, which is less obvious than it sounds. If you're not going to use ice, you need to make sure that you're using the right measurements to fill your glass, all the way to the top, without wastage. This is an art. Change the given measurements as required.

You can top your milkshake with whatever your heart desires. It could be whipped cream, sprinkles, syrups, honey or even sparklers.

Let's start with three versions of a **Strawberry Milkshake** (page 114), and then move on. By the way, to make a **Chocolate Milkshake**, I recommend using **Strawberry Milkshake #3** with a few simple adjustments. Just replace the strawberry ice cream with chocolate ice cream and add a squirt of chocolate syrup. For a **Vanilla Milkshake**, use vanilla ice cream and add vanilla extract.

Strawberry Milkshake #1

Makes 1 drink

Ingredients
250–375 ml milk
200 g hulled strawberries
2 teaspoons sugar or honey, to taste

Preparation
+   Place all the ingredients in a blender, blend until smooth and serve.

Strawberry Milkshake #2

Makes 1 drink

Ingredients
250 ml milk
200 g hulled strawberries
60–90 ml condensed milk
Crushed ice, for blending

Preparation
+   Place all the ingredients in a blender, blend until smooth and serve.

Strawberry Milkshake #3

Makes 1 drink

Ingredients
250 ml milk
2 teaspoons honey, optional
200 g hulled strawberries
2 scoops of vanilla or strawberry ice
    cream (or 1 scoop of each)

Preparation
+   Stir the honey into the milk.
If necessary, dissolve the honey in a little hot water beforehand. Place the honey, milk, strawberries and ice cream in a blender. Blend until smooth and serve.

Jelly Milkshake

Makes 1 drink

Ingredients
125 ml milk
250 ml vanilla ice cream
90 ml flavoured jelly, cut into chunks,
    plus more for garnish

Preparation
+   Place all the ingredients in a blender and blend.
+   Transfer to a glass, top with a few more chunks of jelly, and serve.

Jelly Milkshake

Avocado Shake

Avocado Shake

In India, the avocado is known as the butter fruit. I've tried this recipe many times during avocado season and it only works if your avocado is really soft and ripe. When it does work, it's a very special moment, indeed! An epiphany, really!

Makes 1 drink

Ingredients
½ large, soft, ripe avocado
250 ml milk
½ teaspoon (or less) vanilla extract
Pinch of salt, optional
Pinch of cracked black pepper, optional
Honey, for garnish

Preparation
+   Combine all the ingredients in a blender, and blend until smooth.
+   Transfer to a serving glass, drizzle with honey and serve.

Alternative
Avocado is surprisingly amenable to experimentation and this recipe is easy to adjust if you like. For example, try adding 5–6 hulled strawberries and the zest from half a lemon.

Banana Milkshake

Makes 1 drink

Ingredients
1 tablespoon honey, dissolved in a bit of warm water
250 ml milk
250 ml vanilla ice cream
1 banana

Preparation
+   Combine all the ingredients in a blender, blend until smooth and serve.

Pumpkin Milkshake

Makes 1 drink

Ingredients
110 g tinned pumpkin
250 ml milk
1 teaspoon pure vanilla extract
2 tablespoons honey, or to taste
Pinch of cinnamon
Zest from ½ orange
1-cm (½-inch) piece fresh ginger, peeled and sliced, optional

Preparation
+   Combine all the ingredients in a blender, blend until smooth and serve.

Dried Fruit Milkshake

Of all the milkshakes, this one gets me every time. It absolutely blows me away, is totally and unexpectedly DIVINE, and pretty healthy to boot. I would love to say that I have a perfect recipe, but I tend to change it every time, depending what I find at the market. Don't be afraid to use a lot of fruit and nuts – it will come out really quite thick and gloopy, but the more you use, the tastier it gets. All in all, you should have at least 175 g of your favourite dried fruits and nuts.

The following is merely a suggestion; you should really choose what you like, although I would recommend keeping away from crystallized fruits, which are often packed with preservatives and flavourings. An excellent morning meal, if I do say so myself.

Ingredients

125 ml milk
10 dried pitted dates
3–4 figs
Handful raisins
3–4 prunes
55 g nuts
1 tablespoon honey, or to taste
Pinch of cinnamon, optional
Pinch of nutmeg, optional
Pinch of cardamom powder, optional
1 cm (½-inch) piece fresh ginger, peeled and sliced, optional
Chopped pistachios, for garnish

Preparation

+ Combine all the ingredients in a blender, and blend until smooth.
+ Garnish with pistachios and serve.

Alternative

For an indulgent touch, add 30–60 ml of double cream.

Dried Fruit Milkshake

Tea & Coffee
Mocktails

I think it would be fair to say that not millions, but billions, of us start our day with either tea or coffee. Together, these two rule the world of beverages. Coffee has been around since the 15th century and tea for some 2,500 years before that, although I suspect that both are much older. Both tea and coffee have had, at various times, huge social and cultural influences, as well as associations with religion and ritual. At different times in history, coffee has been banned in countries including Britain, Germany and Ethiopia (to name just a few) for religious and political reasons. We only need to think of the Boston Tea Party to remember that tea has had its era-defining moments as well. I'm normally still half asleep as I bump around the kitchen trying to find my tin of precious coffee and I know that I take this most beloved of treasures for granted on a daily basis. Likewise, tea has nursed me through many a winter (that it was the backbone of the British Empire is of secondary importance!), and I always unthinkingly turn to those most incredible of leaves that nurture so many people the world over when I feel under the weather or a little sorry for myself.

An ongoing debate seems to rage about whether drinking coffee is good for you or not. As with chocolate and wine, we are regularly told that coffee will save us from this, that and the other, only to be 'reliably' informed a week later that it will cause this, that and the other! Perhaps coffee is the less maligned of the three, and in fact, the debate seems to be veering more in the direction of whether coffee actually has any real benefits, rather than whether it is harmful. I could tell experts that my ability to be a functioning member of society largely relies upon coffee, but I'm not sure that would help.

Tea, on the other hand, is mighty good for you. Depending on what kind of tea it is and how you drink it, tea has remarkable antioxidant properties. Antioxidants are the good things that prevent oxidization which, in turn, produces free radicals. Free radicals are not 'good things'. It should be made clear that many so-called herbal teas are not teas at all, and while they may have benefits of their own, the term herbal tea is a huge misnomer, although it is far too late to correct that here. This chapter is about involving these two popular beverages in our experimentation. I adore coffee. Why not see if it goes with something else I adore? Do you like chamomile tea? Who says you have to drink it on its own? Who says it has to be hot? Why not try something a little bit different? If it doesn't work for you, your regular cup of tea or coffee will still be there, waiting patiently.

Autumnal Tea

This drink is tricky to get right and depends entirely on achieving just the right balance between the ingredients. When you do, you'll get a subtle, aromatic drink, whose layers seem to grow as you drink it. Your pear needs to be nice and ripe, so its flavour doesn't get lost. Keep in mind that if the pear can't be muddled, you know it's not ripe enough! The passion fruit should be as sweet as possible, so its natural sourness doesn't dominate.

As for the tea, well, that's the key to it all really; if it's too weak, it will simply dilute the recipe to nothingness; if it's too strong, the bergamot – that distinctive citrus flavour used to make Earl Grey tea – will be overbearing. You can use other types of tea if you like, but aromatic Earl Grey lends itself beautifully to a recipe that reminds me of the flavours of summer's end.

Ingredients

1 ripe pear
1 passion fruit
120 ml Earl Grey tea, cold
15 ml freshly squeezed
      lemon juice
15 ml Sugar Syrup (page 12)
Ice, for shaking and serving
1 pear slice, for garnish

Preparation

+   Muddle the pear in the base of the shaker.
+   Scoop the flesh out of the passion fruit and add to the shaker.
+   Add the tea, lemon juice, sugar syrup and lots of ice, and shake vigorously.
+   Strain into a glass filled with ice, garnish with a slice of pear and serve.

Autumnal Tea

Rooibos Tea & Pomegranate

Mocktails

Rooibos (Rooibosch or Red Bush) Tea & Pomegranate

I must confess that I often find herbal teas rather disappointing. Their glorious smell often belies an insipid, tasteless liquid that leaves me feeling as if I lack appreciation for subtlety. However, there are some herbal teas that do give me the taste kick I'm looking for, and one of those is the marvelous rooibos, with its earthy, nutty, grassy, almost smoky notes. While a cup of rooibos tea is all well and good, I sometimes like to jazz it up, especially if I feel like a cold drink. I love the way that the flavours seem to compete in the mouth, making for a real depth of taste.

Rooibos is gloriously high in antioxidants and is currently being researched as a treatment for acne. Wish I'd known that when I was a teenager!

Makes 1 drink

Ingredients
120 ml strong rooibos tea, cooled
60 ml freshly pressed pomegranate juice
Dash of freshly squeezed lime juice
1 teaspoon honey
Pomegranate seeds, for garnish

Preparation
+   Place all the ingredients in a shaker, and shake vigorously.
+   Strain into a glass, garnish with pomegranate seeds and serve.

Alternatives

Hibiscus & Pomegranate

One of the other herbal teas you might catch me drinking is the elegant hibiscus, which has a fruity, tangy, flowery thing going on. While rooibos and pomegranate may be a more boisterous pairing, hibiscus and pomegranate are calmer together. Follow the recipe on the left, simply substituting hibiscus for rooibos. You'll often find that hibiscus is paired with rose hip when used in a tea, and this also works in this recipe. Hibiscus is a gentle diuretic and a good source of vitamin C. It has also been shown to help lower blood pressure. You can use hibiscus calyces or sepals to make your own hibiscus drink .

Earl Grey Tea & Orange Juice

Here's another nice combination. Replace the rooibos tea with Earl Grey, and the pomegranate juice with orange juice. Garnish with orange slices.

Iced Tea

Iced tea is one of those things that seems so simple that it's almost impossible to write about. It's like telling someone how to boil an egg. Many families have their own method for making iced tea, so let's keep this as simple as it should be. If your family likes iced tea, it's something you want in the fridge all summer long, and to be honest, with all the best intentions in the world, it's probably something you want to be able to make quickly and consistently. It's purely for this reason that I advocate the use of tea bags. Purists may gasp, and if you have the time and leisure, then by all means use tea leaves. But if it's something you make every day, tea bags are so much easier. Just try and get a good brand of tea. We're not talking cars here, and spending just a little extra on a good tea will get you a much better result.

There seems to be two distinct camps when it comes to making iced tea: those who leave the teabags in to steep; and those who take them out before they over steep. Due to the natural tannins in the tea, steeping the teabag too much can make the tea rather bitter and cloudy. Some people like these qualities, so decide what you like, and go for it! Also, remember that the exact quantities are completely up to you. Some people like their ice tea to be quite sweet, whereas others do not.

Ingredients
2 L water
100 g sugar, to taste
5–8 tea bags, to taste

Preparation
+   Pour the water into a medium pan and bring to the boil. When the water boils, remove it from the heat, add the sugar and stir until the water is absolutely clear. Add the tea bags, cover the pot and let the tea steep for 10 minutes. While you're waiting for the water to boil, fill your serving pitcher with hot tap water to temper it.
+   Discard the tea bags from the pot and pour the warm water out of the serving pitcher. Pour the tepid tea into the pitcher and refrigerate until ready to serve.

Arnold Palmer

Named after Arnold Palmer, one the greatest players in golfing history, this is one of the most popular and most well-known mocktails. When made well, it really is a great drink: simple, refreshing and very tasty. Unfortunately, when made badly, it's appalling. In fact, it is such a simple drink that unless you have good basic ingredients, it won't turn out right. You need good iced tea and good lemonade – nothing more, nothing less.

Alternatives

Mint & Jasmine

Use jasmine tea instead of regular tea and add a hearty handful of fresh mint leaves along with the tea bags. Make sure you remove the mint when you remove the tea bags, since mint also has a tendency to turn bitter. When serving, fill the glass with mint leaves and ice before adding the tea.

Lemon & Ginger

I like to add lemon rind and smashed ginger to this tea while the water is still hot, so that the flavours have time to infuse. You can serve the tea immediately over ice, but this will cause the taste to be diluted by the ice, which will throw the balance of the recipe a bit off kilter. Unless you've made the tea stronger for this purpose, I recommend refrigerating before serving. As I mentioned, you can use loose tea leaves rather than tea bags to make iced tea, but then you'll have to strain the tea before pouring it into the pitcher. Some people like to add a pinch of baking soda as soon as the water has boiled and before adding the tea. This acts against the tannins in the tea and prevents the tea from becoming bitter or cloudy. Obviously, you can experiment with all kinds of flavoured teas, as well as with extra ingredients. For example, try making Earl Grey Iced Tea with slices of lemon and orange.

Makes 1 drink

Ingredients
120 ml Iced Tea (page 128)
120 ml Lemonade (page 28)
Ice, for serving
Slice of lemon, for garnish

Preparation
+   Pour the iced tea and lemonade in a glass over ice and stir.
+   Garnish with a slice of lemon and serve.

Alternative
You could use flavoured tea for this drink, but out of respect to Mr. Palmer, I'll just throw the idea out there and let you do what you want. If you do decide to experiment, give it a different name.

Earl Grey & Grape Cobbler

There's an old-school cocktail recipe that dates back to about 1840 and is called a cobbler. I say this to stress that we are not talking about baked goods here. The cobbler recipe is very simple; what makes it special as a cocktail is its presentation and this is the idea I have in mind here. If anything, this mocktail is more of a serving suggestion than an actual recipe and you can adapt the style to suit all kinds of colour and fruit.

A cobbler should be served in a goblet, which is a glass vessel often mistaken for a wine glass. A goblet is, in fact, slightly bigger than a wine glass. It's also thicker and heavier.

You could use a wine glass if that's all you have, but wine glasses are a bit too delicate. A good goblet has a nice weight to it that suits the recipe much better.

Garnish is key to the cobbler. It was the first cocktail that was served not only with a drinking straw (straws were considered a great novelty when they first appeared, as described in Charles Dickens' Martin Chuzzlewit of 1844),

Ingredients
90 ml strong Earl Grey tea
1 teaspoon sugar
1 lemon wedge
Fresh fruit salad (chopped peaches, grapes, mangoes, pomegranate seeds, kiwi, etc.)
Mint leaves, for garnish
Crushed ice, for garnish

Preparation
+   Combine the tea and sugar, squeeze in the lemon wedge, and set aside to cool.
+   Transfer the mixture to a goblet and garnish with fruit salad and mint leaves.
+   Fill the cup with crushed ice, add a straw and a long-handled spoon, top with more garnish and serve.

Alternatives
*   You can really play around with this idea. Raspberries are a great fruit for muddling and they are a delicious replacement for the fruit salad in the above recipe. Use chamomile tea instead of Earl Grey tea and garnish the concoction with a few more raspberries. You might want to mix fruit syrups with your teas.
*   Remember to make the tea strong, as it will have to stand up to the fruit as well as being diluted by the ice.

Earl Grey & Grape Cobbler

Chai Masala

The word chai in the West has now come to mean what is more properly known as Masala chai, while in Hindi chai refers more generally to tea. The associations that go with this small word are truly enormous. Masala chai has become very popular in recent years and many coffee chains serve their own version of it. There is even the popular Chai Latte, but I won't get into that here.

Masala chai is really very simple to make and can be adapted to suit your personal taste with very little effort. Most Indian stores stock several Masala mix versions for chai, so this is a great starting point. As always, I recommend that you experiment until you find what makes your mouth and belly happiest (shouldn't that be true of all cooking and beverage making?!).

Ingredients

375 ml water
½ cinnamon stick
Pinch of grated fresh ginger
5–6 cardamom pods, cracked
8 cloves
½ teaspoon fennel seeds
Pinch of cracked black pepper, plus more for serving
Pinch of grated nutmeg
1 bay leaf, optional
750 ml milk
4–6 teaspoons honey or light brown sugar, to taste
2–3 teaspoons Assam, Darjeeling or Mamr tea leaves
Ice, optional

Alternatives

* Condensed milk can add a richness that some people love. Remember that condensed milk is sweet (60 ml of condensed milk is equivalent to about 2 tablespoons of sugar in terms of sweetness), so if you decide to include it, you may want to reduce the amount of honey or sugar you use.
* Consider adding a splash of rosewater for an extra, interesting layer of aroma.
* Once you perfect your recipe, try to make your own spice mix and pare down the quantities so that you can make one cup at a time.

Preparation

+ Place the water, cinnamon, ginger, cardamom, cloves, fennel seeds, black pepper, nutmeg and bay leaf in a small pan and bring to a boil.
+ Cover and simmer for 10 minutes
+ Add the milk and honey, and bring back to a boil.
+ Remove from the heat and add the tea leaves. Cover and set aside for a few minutes.
+ Strain and then serve warm or chilled over ice with a sprinkle of black pepper.

Thai Tea

Makes about 2 L

Ingredients

2 L water
100 g sugar, to taste
5–8 tea bags, to taste
2 teaspoons mix of spices (such as
    star anise, fennel seed, cardamom,
    cinnamon, nutmeg, vanilla, ground
    tamarind and ground ginger) or Thai
    tea mix, to taste
125 ml condensed milk, plus more
    for serving
Ice, for serving
Evaporated milk or coconut, optional

Preparation

+   Pour the water into a medium pan
and bring to the boil. While you're
waiting for the water to boil, fill your
serving pitcher with hot tap water to
temper it.

+   When the water boils, remove it from
the heat, add the sugar and stir until the
water is absolutely clear. Add the tea bags
(make sure you use enough tea bags to
make the tea very strong) and the spice
mix, cover the pot and let the tea steep
for 10 minutes. Discard the tea bags and
strain the tea. Stir in the condensed milk,
then transfer the tea to the refrigerator
and chill. To serve, pour the chilled tea
into glasses filled with ice, leaving a bit of
room at the top.

+   Fill the rest of the glass with evaporated
milk and serve without stirring.

Bandrek

Makes about 1 L

Ingredients

1.25 L water
85–175 g mashed ginger
100–150 g palm sugar, honey or white
    sugar, to taste
1 cinnamon stick
5–60 mloves
2 pandan leaves or 1 teaspoon
    pandan essence
2 stalks lemongrass, bottom halves,
    smashed
2 pinches of salt
1 star anise, optional
5 cardamom pods, cracked, optional
½ teaspoon coriander seeds, optional
½–1 dried hot chilli pepper, optional
½ vanilla pod, split open, or a few drops
    vanilla extract, optional
80 g shredded fresh coconut (about
    1 coconut), optional

Preparation

+   Put the water, ginger, sugar,
cinnamon, cloves, pandan, lemongrass,
salt and the optional flavourings of your
choice into a large pot. Bring to a boil and
then simmer for about 15 minutes. The
longer you simmer, the more the liquid
will reduce and the more intense the
flavours will be.

+   Strain and serve.

Iced Coffee

Maybe it has something to do with global warming, but iced coffee seems to be more and more popular every year. The problem is that so much of it is just dreadful! There is all manner of rubbish available from frozen or slushy type dispensers, and I often suspect that these concoctions have never seen coffee beans in their life. Alternately, people simply pour instant coffee over some ice and call that an iced coffee, a crime which should really be considered a criminal offence! I don't even approve of using espresso, cold milk and ice for iced coffee. (Indeed, it's possible that I just shouldn't drink iced coffee, isn't it?!)

Here are two versions that I have used in the past. I confess that these are easier to make in a bar, where you have a big coffee machine at your disposal. But whatever you do, please don't use instant coffee!

Iced Coffee

The element in this recipe that really sets it apart is the double cream, which adds richness and flavour. Obviously, you can leave it out, but to really experience the drink, I recommend including it. As for the milk, though it may seem a bit odd to heat it and then cool it, the fact of the matter is that steamed or boiled milk has a slightly different taste and texture to regular milk. This adds another dimension to the recipe.

Makes 1 drink

Ingredients

1 single or double espresso
6–90 ml milk, steamed and cooled
30 ml Sugar Syrup (page 12) or
    flavoured syrup
15–30 ml double cream, optional
Ice, for shaking and serving

Preparation

+   Pour the espresso, cooled milk, sugar syrup, double cream and ice into a shaker, and shake vigorously.
+   Pour into a glass with ice and serve.

Café Bon Bon Style

Though it's tempting to make iced coffee sweet, be careful not to make it too sweet. Since this version is blended with ice, you'll need some extra sweetness, or it may taste over-diluted. Flavoured syrups are a delicious addition. There is actually a (lesser known) way of serving espresso, which is known as Café Bon Bon, and this recipe is adapted from that yummy beverage.

Makes 1 drink

Ingredients

1 single or double espresso
60 ml condensed milk
Splash of milk
30 ml flavoured syrup, optional
Crushed ice, for blending

Preparation

+   Place the espresso, condensed milk, milk and syrup in a blender.
+   Add just enough crushed ice so that it reaches the top of the liquid, blend until smooth and serve.

Iced Spiced Turkish Coffee

Makes 1 drink

My coffee of choice is Turkish coffee (also known as Greek and Armenian coffee, among other names); it's the one with the sludge in the bottom. I'm utterly addicted and actually have to limit myself to the number of cups I drink in a day. Cooking Turkish coffee is an art. I've given some basic instructions in this recipe, but mastering the technique can take quite a long time (and a lot of messy stove tops, too). Turkish coffee isn't right for regular iced coffee, but it is perfect for the drink described below, especially if you flavour it with all manner of spices.

If the thought of making Turkish coffee terrifies you (and it might), then use a double espresso instead. Alternatively, you can cheat by using the following method: Pour boiling water directly over very finely ground coffee beans, stir, and leave it to settle. Gently pour off the coffee without disturbing the sediment at the bottom of the cup and use this to make your iced coffee drink.

Ingredients

120 ml water
Pinch of ground nutmeg
Pinch of ground or grated ginger
3–5 cardamom pods, cracked
A few cloves
Pinch of fennel seeds or ½ star anise
Pinch of ground cinnamon
1 teaspoon white sugar, or to taste
1 heaping teaspoon Turkish coffee
Ice, for serving
Milk or double cream, for serving, optional

Preparation

+   Put the water in a narrow tall pan. A specially-made Cezve or Ibrik* is ideal. Stir in the nutmeg, ginger, cardamom, cloves, fennel seeds, cinnamon and sugar, and heat over medium to high heat.

+   When the water starts steaming, sprinkle the coffee over the top, so that it totally covers the surface of the water. Resist the temptation to stir.
+   As the water begins to boil, it will push through what is now a coffee crust. Let it. When the coffee starts to rise, much like boiling milk, remove it immediately from the heat and allow to settle for a moment.
+   Return to the heat, allow the coffee to rise again, and then remove. Repeat for a third time.
+   Allow the coffee to cool, and then strain very well into a glass with ice. Top with milk or double cream, and serve.

*Ceve and Ibrik are just two of the names for the specially designed vessel made for cooking this kind of coffee.

Iced Spiced Turkish Coffee

Coffee
& Mango

I learned about mixing coffee and mango from a fantastic and innovative chef I once worked with. I thought he was a bit crazy the first time he recommended it; however, after more persuasion, I opened my mind and gave it a try. Needless to say, I was pleasantly surprised. There is obviously a lesson to be learned here and I urge you too to keep an open mind. Try everything. If you have an idea, go with it.

If there are two ingredients that you love, however disparate they may be, they may work fantastically together. Who knows? Of course, they may not, but a mistake is just as valuable a lesson as a success. Sermon is now over. From what I can gather, this blend originates from Pakistan, although I may be wrong! Anyway, this is my adaptation.

If you don't want to use condensed milk, use about 60–90 ml of milk and 30 ml of Sugar Syrup (see page 12).

Ingredients
100 g mango cubes
1 double espresso
30 ml milk
60 ml condensed milk
Ice, for serving
Whipped cream, for garnish

Preparation
+   Combine all the ingredients in a blender, and blend until smooth.
+   Pour into a glass over ice, garnish with whipped cream and serve.

Alternatives
*   This drink is also fantastic when served blended. Make sure you use crushed ice, rather than ice cubes, and add chunks of mango for garnish.
*   Be careful about mixing coffee with fruit. Coffee is bitter and many fruits are naturally sour; combining the two can sometimes be unpalatable.
*   I have tried variations on this drink with some success and am happy to impart what I have learnt. Lychee and passion fruit work well; so do cherries if you're in the right mood. You could also add some double cream into the mix if you wished.

Coffee & Mango

Iced Mocha Coffee

As a bartender, I have nearly boiled over when asked to make one of these. Once, through a clenched jaw, I harrumphed loudly and pompously pronounced that I do not work at a coffee chain. At the same time, you wouldn't catch me ordering one of these from a coffee chain, as I balk at the idea of spending a small fortune on a chocolatey coffee.

However, there's no denying that coffee and chocolate are a perfect match. And this is one recipe in which I go against my usual principles – of using so-called real ingredients. In fact, you can't use real chocolate for one of these drinks, as all sorts of dreadful lumpy things happen when real chocolate and ice are mixed, and I never have the patience (or quite frankly the skill) to make decent chocolate syrup. Besides, it's not like we're trying to be healthy here, is it? What I'm saying is, go buy yourself some good chocolate syrup.

Ingredients

125 ml strong black coffee or 1 double espresso
125 ml milk
2 teaspoons brown sugar, or to taste
1 tablespoon chocolate syrup, plus more
    for garnish
Dash vanilla extract
Crushed ice, for blending
Whipped cream, for garnish
Grated chocolate, for garnish

Preparation

+   Put the coffee, milk, brown sugar, chocolate syrup, vanilla extract and crushed ice in a blender, and blend until smooth.
+   Pour into a glass, garnish with whipped cream, chocolate syrup or grated chocolate (or all three!), and serve.

Alternatives

⋆   I often find that when you blend coffee with ice, it dilutes the taste too much. One solution is to freeze strong black coffee in an ice cube tray and use it to blend the iced coffee. Genius!
⋆   If you aren't too worried about calories (or even if you are, but like to indulge), replace the sugar with 60 ml of condensed milk. It might just tip you over the edge, so be warned.
⋆   If you are going to garnish with whipped cream, it should go without saying that you should prepare it beforehand. (I didn't really need to say that, did I?)

Soda Mocktails

In 1767, Joseph Priestly, one of the great thinkers of 18th-century Britain, discovered soda water. In the 19th century, the soda fountain appeared in the United States, and generations of dentists and dieticians have been busy ever since. While liquors, beers, wines and cocktails come and go with the seasons, plain old soda water has been my most constant companion in my many years behind the bar. A glass full of soda water, sometimes with lime and Angostura bitters, is never far from my reach. I must have drunk lakefuls of the stuff. I love those bubbles that seem to perk me up and help my food go down. It is endlessly versatile and an essential ingredient of any bar, bringing life to many a recipe.

Add something sweet and those bubbles can keep both children and adults happy and entertained for an eternity. I have tried not to lecture about health benefits and warnings in previous chapters and have no intention of doing so here. We all know the dangers of soda pop, as well as how good it can taste. Just as you should be wary of drinking too much beetroot juice, you should also avoid drinking too much cola or lemon-lime soda, albeit for rather different reasons. As I have said before, my concern is taste. Responsibility regarding the recommended amounts for consumption is in your hands.

There are an endless variety of sodas available on the market these days, with a flavour for each day of the year. In this chapter, I have tried to give you a few recipes to show you that you can play around with soda pop as much as with other ingredients. Some are old-school recipes that hark back to the days of the soda fountain, while others give you ideas on how to make your own flavoured sodas. Again, there are a million and one flavours out there. Use these recipes as a basis or template to expand on. Just one final word of warning: sodas and their bubbles have more potential for making sticky messes than any other type of drinks.I claim no responsibility whatsoever for the tidiness and well-being of your kitchen or bar if you decide to try these recipes!

Shirley Temple

Perhaps the Shirley Temple is the original mocktail, invented for the child film star of the same name. Temple's movie career was all of eight years long, from the age of four until twelve. She made a few films in her teens, but these were received with partial or little success. Still, at the height of her fame, she was a huge star, perhaps the biggest box office draw of the mid-1930s. She retired from the industry at the age of 22 and went on to have a successful diplomatic career.

Today, the Shirley Temple isn't perceived as a particularly exciting drink, although we should pay it some respect for working hard for so many years. What I find extraordinary is that for such a famous drink, there seems to be so much confusion over the recipe! I can understand recipe confusions where alcohol is involved, but mocktails are supposed to keep your head clear!

Ingredients

60 ml freshly squeezed orange juice
120 ml ginger ale
Splash of Homemade Grenadine (page 15)
Pomegranate seeds or a maraschino cherry,
    for garnish
Ice, for serving, optional

Preparation

+   Pour the orange juice, ginger ale and grenadine syrup into a tall glass.
+   Garnish with pomegranate seeds, for a contemporary look, or with a maraschino cherry. Add ice if you like, and serve.

Alternatives

Today you are more likely to get a drink made of ginger ale and lemon, lime soda with grenadine, or maybe even orange juice, lemon-lime soda and grenadine. I must confess, I find it rather sad that the recipe, whatever its merits, seems to have been forgotten. One more thing – my aversion to cheap maraschino cherries normally drives me to garnish this drink with a wedge or wheel of lime instead.

Shirley Temple

Roy Rogers

Another well-known mocktail was named for the King of the Cowboys, beloved actor and singer Roy Rogers. It's not the most imaginative drink in the world, but here it is, for the record.

Makes 1 drink

Ingredients
Ice, for serving
Cola
Splash of Homemade Grenadine
    (page 15)
Maraschino cherry, for garnish

Preparation
+   Place the ice in a tall glass.
+   Top with cola and grenadine syrup.
+   Garnish with a maraschino cherry and serve.

Brown Cow

When I was a kid, my friends and I aspired to a Brown Cow. We would save up our pennies to buy them – never more than once a week. It was a deluxe type of treat. I must confess that I haven't had one for a very long time, and to be honest, I don't think I want to. It's one of those things that is so etched into my memory, I'm almost scared to make one now and not like it. So this really is a drink from my memory.

Makes 1 drink

Ingredients
2 scoops of vanilla ice cream
250 ml cola or root beer
1 vanilla pod, for garnish

Preparation
+   Put 1 scoop of ice cream in the bottom of a glass and pour in the cola.
+   Stir a bit, then add the second scoop of ice cream and serve.
+   Garnish with a vanilla pod and serve.

Alternatives
*   Use chocolate ice cream instead of vanilla ice cream to make a **Chocolate Cow**.
*   Use ginger ale instead of cola and blend the ingredients to make a **Boston Cooler**.

Brown Cow

Egg Cream

Egg Cream

This was another soda fountain favourite. Believe it or not, there was actually a time when it was made with eggs and cream, along with syrup and soda, similar to old-fashioned milkshakes. The recipe has changed over time and oddly enough, Egg Cream is now a drink with contains neither eggs nor cream.

Makes 1 drink

Ingredients
60 ml excellent quality
  chocolate syrup
60 ml cold milk
Soda water or seltzer water

Preparation
+   Pour the chocolate syrup into a glass and then pour in the milk, stirring until combined.
+   Add soda water until the glass is about half filled, and stir. The mixture should start to foam up.
+   Continue adding soda water, stirring all the time, encouraging the foam to rise, until the glass is full and the drink is impressive.
+   Serve immediately. If the foam has been made properly, a straw will be able to stand straight up.

Elderberry Cordial

Elderberries and elderflowers are amazingly tasty and aromatic, and their cordial can be used in everything from beverages to pancake toppings. You might have to go and find the berries for yourself, since buying them at your local grocer can be difficult, but you're likely to find both flowers and berries available if you're willing to search a bit.

Yield depends on size of bucket

Ingredients
Elderberries (up to a bucketful)
Water
Cloves, optional
Sugar, white or brown, to taste

Preparation
+   Place the elderberries in a large pan and add enough water to cover.
+   Bring the mixture to the boil and simmer for about 30 minutes.
+   Pour the mixture through muslin to strain, and then return the liquid to the pan.
+   Add 5 cloves and 500 g of sugar for every 500 ml of liquid. Bring the mixture to a boil and boil for at least 10 minutes, stirring occasionally.
+   Let the mixture cool, then transfer to sterilized glass bottles and seal with a plastic or rubber cap.

Flavoured Water

The basic idea behind making natural flavoured water is to fill a pitcher with water, add flavourings and let them sit in the water as it chills, so that the water takes on their flavour. Of course, whether you use tap water, filtered water or bottled mineral water is entirely up to you. The recipes below are meant to give you ideas, but you can really use your imagination. Combine a couple of the suggestions below, such as cucumber and mint, or create something that's entirely your own.

Cucumber Flavoured Water

Slice a cucumber in long thin strips, or use a vegetable peeler to peel long strips, and place the strips in a pitcher filled with water. This is one of my favourites, and you'll be surprised at what a difference it makes.

Mint Flavoured Water

Thoroughly wash a handful of fresh mint and place in a pitcher filled of water. You can use lemon verbena, lemon balm, or any other type of mint that you like. You can use a blend of mints if you like.

Citrus Flavoured Water

I don't like slices of lemon in my water. It gives such a stringy taste and after a while, the slices start to look unattractive. However, the rind citrus fruit, such as lime, lemon, orange and grapefruit, is packed with aromatic oil that imbue water an amazing taste and smell. Use a vegetable peeler to remove strips of lemon rind (try not to include any white pith) and add them to a pitcher filled with water. The longer you leave the rinds, the better. You can use one citrus fruit per pitcher or combine several together. Consider adding a strand of saffron for a touch of the exotic.

Ginger Flavoured Water

It may not be to everyone's liking, but ginger makes me a very happy fellow indeed. You can add thin strips of peeled ginger, or even smashed ginger, to your water. I also recommend adding ginger to any of the above flavoured water recipes.

Flavoured Water

Vanilla Syrup

There are all types of syrups on the market which can be used for cocktails, coffees and flavoured sodas. The range of quality is quite staggering, even within the same brand, and a certain amount of trial and error is required until you find just what you're looking for. For example, one company may produce great grenadine syrup but lousy vanilla syrup. Another option, of course, is making your own syrups and cordials (as demonstrated in the recipe on page 151).

Makes about 300 ml

Ingredients
2–3 vanilla pods
250 ml water
200 g sugar

Preparation
+   Slice open the vanilla pods and scrape out the insides with the back of a knife. Mix the vanilla seeds, the empty pods and the sugar together, and store in an airtight container for as long as possible (up to a week is recommended).
+   Place the water in a small saucepan and add the vanilla sugar. Heat gently over low heat, stirring until all the sugar is dissolved. Strain and use.

Lavender & Lemon Syrup

Lavender is making a comeback. For a long time it was confined to the bathroom, in the form of air fresheners, but its popularity in aromatherapy has resulted in its return to other rooms of the house, including the kitchen. You can use all parts of the lavender plant as flavouring, but I recommend using the flowers and buds, firstly because it lends a fantastic hue to the syrup, and secondly because the stems and leaves.

Makes about 300 ml

Ingredients
Rind from 1–2 lemons
10 lavender flower heads
250 ml warm water
200 g sugar

Preparation
+   Place the lemon rind, lavender and water in a small pot and let stand for a few hours at room temperature.
+   Add the sugar and then heat gently, stirring all the time, until the sugar dissolves. Strain and transfer to an airtight container with a tight-fitting lid.

Serving suggestion
To serve, pour about 1 tablespoon of syrup into a glass and top with sparkling water.

Lavender & Lemon Syrup

Homemade Soda

By now, you may have realized that I like to play around in the kitchen and try new things. My approach is to keep an open mind and palate. Sadly, it is this attitude that led to the early demise of my beloved soda siphon. I was experimenting with making carbonated drinks from all kinds of ingredients and was unaware that this was causing fatal damage to the inner workings of said siphon. Before I realized my mistake, my siphon had passed on to that great scrap heap of bar paraphernalia in the sky.

So the moral of this tale is: never put anything other than water in your soda siphon. Home soda makers works a bit differently, and makes it entirely possible to create do-it-yourself sodas. You can make these with any type of homemade or store-bought syrup. Just mix the syrup with water and make it fizzy. Hours of experimenting can be enjoyed in this area, especially if you are inspired by the previous syrup recipes (page 154). Alternately, use something that is not concentrated, such as apple juice. If you have freshly pressed apple juice or grape juice on hand and want to alter it without diluting it, try invigorating it with a home soda maker.

Some fruit juices are not great when carbonated. These tend to be thicker juices that don't take on the bubbles so readily. Thicker juice with bubbles can also leave a bizarre feeling in the mouth. However, I encourage you to look through the recipes in this book, choose one, strain the drink well and then attempt to make it fizzy. The flavored waters mentioned in this chapter are perfect candidates, as in the Autumnal Tea (page 124). Indeed, tea is one of my favorite things to carbonate. It tends to be thinner in body than juices and with a little help, is very tasty when carbonated. Fizzy tea is definitely not something you'll find readily in your supermarket. Here are a few suggestions to get you going.

Chamomile Soda

Makes 1 drink

Ingredients

250 ml strong chamomile tea, hot
Handful mint leaves
1 lime wedge
15–30 ml Elderflower Cordial
  (page 151)
Ice, for shaking
Mint sprigs, for garnish

Preparation

+   Mix the mint leaves into the hot tea and then set aside to cool.
+   Transfer the tea to the refrigerator and chill.
+   Pour the chilled tea into a shaker, squeeze in the lime, and then add the cordial and ice. Shake vigorously.
+   Strain and carbonate. Garnish with mint and serve.

Earl Grey Soda

Makes 1 drink

Ingredients

250 ml strong Earl Grey tea, chilled
1 lime wedge
1 orange wedge
15–30 ml Elderflower Cordial
  (page 151), to taste
Ice, for shaking
Orange slice, for garnish

Preparation

+   Place the tea in a shaker.
+   Squeeze in the lime wedge and orange wedge, add the cordial and ice, and shake vigorously.
+   Strain and carbonate.
+   Garnish with a slice of orange and serve.

Hibiscus Soda

Hibiscus Soda

Makes 1 drink

Ingredients

1-cm (½-inch) piece fresh ginger, peeled
    and sliced
2 cloves, smashed
15–30 ml Vanilla Syrup
    (page 154)
250 ml strong hibiscus tea, hot
Ice, for shaking and serving

Preparation

+ Smash the ginger in the base of a
shaker. Transfer to a cup and mix in the
cloves, vanilla syrup and hot tea.
+ Set aside to cool and then transfer to
the refrigerator to chill.
+ Pour the chilled tea into a shaker, add
ice and shake vigorously.
+ Strain, carbonate and serve in a glass
filled with ice.

Soda Royale

*It's not a great name, I know, and not
even a correct one, so if you can think of
a better name, I urge you to use it! This
is meant to be a take on the Kir Royale,
a cocktail consisting of champagne and
Crème de Cassis.*

Makes 1 drink

Ingredients

90 ml soda or sparkling mineral water
30 ml pressed blackberry juice
30 ml pressed white grape juice
Sugar Syrup (page 12), optional
Blackberry, for garnish

Preparation

+ Combine the soda, blackberry juice
and grape juice in a champagne glass.
+ Add a dash of sugar syrup if you want,
but remember that this isn't meant to be
an overly sweet drink.
+ Garnish with a blackberry and serve.

Alternative

* You can replace the blackberry juice
with almost any other berry juice as long
as it has a reasonably strong character.
* For example, raspberry and
redcurrant juice are great alternatives.
Be aware of natural sugar levels.

Index